Portrait of the
West Somerset
Railway

Portrait of the
West Somerset
Railway

25 YEARS OF PRESERVATION PROGRESS

ALAN STANISTREET

First published 1996

ISBN 0 7110 2487 1

Published by Ian Allan Ltd

an imprint of Ian Allan Ltd,
Terminal House, Station Approach,
Shepperton, Surrey TW17 8AS.
Printed by Ian Allan Printing Ltd,
Coombelands House,
Coombelands Lane, Addlestone,
Weybridge, Surrey KT15 1HY.

Below: On 1 May 1993 the Cravens-built two-car DMU
formed the 15.40 Watchet-Minehead train. It is pictured
at Kentsford. *Stephen Edge*

Front cover: Ex-GWR 2-6-2T No 5572 approaches
Crowcombe with the 10.00 from Minehead on 24 August
1986. *Mick Roberts*

Back cover, top: Victor waits to return to Minehead from
Blue Anchor on re-opening day, 28 March 1976.
Allan Stanistreet

Back cover, bottom: The Association Permanent Way gang
seen removing the siding point at Blue Anchor in 1975.
Allan Stanistreet

About the Author

Allan Stanistreet has been a member of the West
Somerset Railway Association since 1974 and a
shareholder in the company since 1976. An active
volunteer over the years, he wrote the first official
guide to the line, the text for the first *Stations and
Building* book and was the founder editor of the
WSR Journal in 1978.

Born in 1940, he spent 30 years in the army,
retiring in 1988. He is now an Executive Officer in
the Civil Service. Married in 1967, he has three
grown-up children.

Other interests include researching the recipients
of gallantry awards and rallying his vintage Fordson
tractor (including participation in 'Friends of
Thomas the Tank Engine' weekends). This is his
fourth published book.

Contents

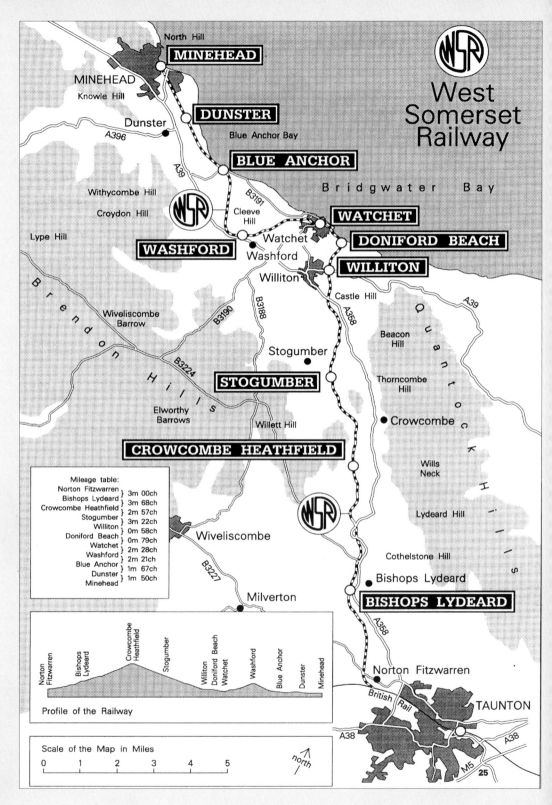

West Somerset Railway

North Hill

MINEHEAD

MINEHEAD
Knowle Hill

Dunster
A396

A39

DUNSTER

Blue Anchor Bay

BLUE ANCHOR

B3191

Bridgwater Bay

Withycombe Hill

Croydon Hill

Cleeve Hill

WATCHET

Lype Hill

Watchet

WASHFORD

Washford

DONIFORD BEACH

Williton

WILLITON

Castle Hill

A39

Wiveliscombe Barrow

B3190

B3188

A358

Beacon Hill

Brendon Hills

Stogumber

Thorncombe Hill

B3224

Quantock Hills

Elworthy Barrows

STOGUMBER

Willett Hill

Crowcombe

CROWCOMBE HEATHFIELD

Wills Neck

Mileage table:

Norton Fitzwarren	3m 00ch
Bishops Lydeard	3m 68ch
Crowcombe Heathfield	2m 57ch
Stogumber	3m 22ch
Williton	0m 58ch
Doniford Beach	0m 79ch
Watchet	2m 28ch
Washford	2m 21ch
Blue Anchor	1m 67ch
Dunster	1m 50ch
Minehead	

Lydeard Hill

Wiveliscombe

Cothelstone Hill

B3227

Milverton

Bishops Lydeard

BISHOPS LYDEARD

A358

Norton Fitzwarren

British Rail

TAUNTON

A38

A38

M5

25

Profile of the Railway

Norton Fitzwarren — Bishops Lydeard — Crowcombe Heathfield — Stogumber — Williton — Doniford Beach — Watchet — Washford — Blue Anchor — Dunster — Minehead

Scale of the Map in Miles

0 1 2 3 4 5

north

Foreword *by Bill Pertwee*

There are certain branch lines within our rail network that have appealed to the public slightly more than others. Many of them received the 'Beeching axe' in the 1960s, some even before that.

I was lucky to travel on some of them when they were part of British Rail and before the system was nationalised. There are one or two that I dearly wish I had travelled on before they were closed: one was the Somerset & Dorset (which was slightly more than just a branch line, to put it mildly) and another was the Taunton to Minehead.

Luckily, I have had the opportunity to travel on the latter since it was preserved and reopened in 1976 by the West Somerset Railway Co most ably supported by the West Somerset Railway Association.

Bishops Lydeard to Minehead is a delightful journey and one I have done several times. There is just something about the lovely Somerset countryside and the whole experience of stopping at country stations: the quite delightful little Stogumber and Crowcombe, which is still a typical branch line station, where you are greeted by the gentlemanly Walter Harris, just as I suspect passengers were treated by the Stationmaster when it was part of the original branch line. Dunster station always makes me think of past decades and I can imagine people arriving for the polo matches; you can clearly see the polo field today. Then, of course, there is Watchet, which must have seen many a Territorial Army part-timer alighting to start his two-week summer camp in the area.

Finally, you have that long run into Minehead. My wife, who did a summer show at the old Gaiety theatre in the early 1950s in the town, remembers standing on the platform waiting to meet her mother who was coming down to join her for a short stay. She said, 'We all used to say it was like High Noon, seeing the train in the distance coming along the straight into the station.'

How many thousands and thousands of holidaymakers have experienced the sensation of High Noon into Minehead, the friendly guest houses waiting to greet them and eventually the sight of the sands and North Hill in the background?

Here in this book Allan has given us an insight into the whole organisation that brought about the preservation of the 'Branch Line to Minehead', so beloved of so many people in the past and, thank

Above: Actor and author Bill Pertwee enjoys the Taunton 150 celebrations at Bishops Lydeard in 1992.
John Pearce

goodness, restored so that we can enjoy it in the same way today.

I must congratulate him in making me realise just how much hard work has gone into the massive job of preservation for everyone to enjoy and, I am sure, continue to enjoy for many years to come.

Bill Pertwee
September 1995

Class 8F No 48773, normally based on the Severn Valley Railway, approaches Stogumber on 30 April 1993 with a special goods working, which had been organised as a photo charter. *Stephen Edge*

Introduction

The aim of this book is to recount, in words and pictures, the history of the 'new' West Somerset Railway Co from its inception in 1971 to its Silver Jubilee year, 1996. Inextricably linked with this is the history and development of its supporting body, the West Somerset Railway Association. Indeed, without the latter it is probably safe to say that the railway in its present form might not have come into existence and almost certainly would not exist at all today. It is only fitting that due tribute should be paid here to hundreds of volunteers who have given thousands of hours of their time and expertise entirely free of charge to the railway over the last eventful quarter of a century.

Several specialist publications are devoted to different aspects of the line: the *Stock Book* provides a reasonably up-to-date list of locomotives and rolling stock currently to be found on the railway; the *Stations and Buildings Book*, now in its fourth edition, gives precise details of every station and major building on the line, even incorporating useful information for modellers, such as distances and gradient profiles. Lastly, may be mentioned the *Official Guide Book*, which contains, amongst other things, a guided tour of the line. It is therefore

suggested that this present work should be read in conjunction with one or all of these.

I am delighted that Bill Pertwee has kindly consented to write the Foreword for this book. Bill is a staunch supporter of the railway and I am most grateful to him for his interest.

Gratitude is also extended to the following, in alphabetical order, for their ready willingness to provide material and encouragement: Don Bishop, Hein Burger, Ian Coleby, Stephen Edge, Barney Forsdike, Andy Forster, John Glover, Norman Hawkes, Richard Jones, Steve Martin, John Pearce, Eric Rowlands, John Simms, Mark Smith, Peter Thompson.

In conclusion, I make the usual author's declaration that while striving to achieve total accuracy, I realise that unintentional errors may have crept in. The responsibility for these is mine alone.

Allan Stanistreet
February 1996

Below: At the start of a new season GWR Prairie tank No 4561 brings a train into Bishops Lydeard on 4 March 1990. *Peter Thompson*

The West Somerset Railway
1971-1996 *The First 25 Years*

British Railways closed the branch line from Taunton to Minehead as from 2 January 1971. Well before closure by BR, certain interested parties had been investigating ways and means by which the line, the last of the railways round Exmoor, might be kept open. In the very nature of such schemes, optimism abounded; however, it was to be over five long years before regular train services were to run over the line again and even then the promoters were to be denied the goal they originally sought: that of running to and from the main line station at Taunton.

Somerset County Council held a meeting on 5 February 1971 in Taunton for interested parties to consider hardships which might arise from closure and to consider the future. Unlike many other preservation schemes, the line had been left *in situ*, so little or no expensive reinstatement was necessary. However, in the years prior to closure, BR had removed some of the infrastructure. Most stations had become unstaffed halts with tickets sold on the trains; signalling had been reduced to the bare minimum, the loop at Crowcombe (now Crowcombe Heathfield) had been removed and no run-round facilities existed at Minehead. Indeed, the line had been truncated there to terminate well short of the wall adjoining the road where the present buffer stops are situated.

It was decided at this early stage that the railway service should be reinstated throughout the whole

Left: On 17 April 1995 ex-BR(W) 2-6-2-T No 4160 is seen at the Old Cleeve Bridge with the 12.20 service from Bishops Lydeard to Minehead. *Stephen Edge.*

Below: A graphic picture of Minehead during the period of closure from 1971 until 1976. Note how the track ends approximately opposite the door to the 1996 enquiry office. *Eric Rowlands*

Left: Minehead slumbers; the platform signage remains but the track is a weed-strewn wilderness.
Eric Rowlands

Below left: The rusting tracks stretch into the distance; a view looking south at Williton in the early 1970s.
Eric Rowlands

Right: A view of Williton looking north during the period of closure; note the flat-bottomed rail that was put in when the loop was shortened.
Eric Rowlands

length of the line. A working party was formed with two local businessmen at its head: Douglas Fear as Chairman and George Byam-Shaw as Secretary. They were to undertake a feasibility study with regard to reopening the line under private enterprise and their favourable report, published in April 1971, led to the formation of the West Somerset Private Railway Co. The company would raise the necessary finance and conduct negotiations with BR. Messrs Fear and Byam-Shaw became Chairman and Secretary respectively of this new company.

At about the same time as the formation of the company, the West Somerset Railway Association was founded. The objects of the association were threefold:

1. The acquisition, restoration and preservation of interesting items of railway equipment.

2. The affording of facilities to members to assist in the operation of the railway.

3. To form the association into a company, limited by guarantee, with power to invest in the operating company of the railway.

The last was finally achieved in 1995!

The first newsletter published by the association, edited by R. F. Norris and dated July 1971, concluded with the words: 'Let us hope that good sense and reason will prevail and that we shall be able to achieve our objects to the full.' It is probably true to say that this hope has been largely fulfilled.

There are many individuals who are principally interested in pioneering and once something is up and running, they depart for new challenges. This is true of the West Somerset Railway, although it is heartening to record that some of the early

protagonists are still to be seen about the line.

Inevitably, the prospect of reopening the line provoked strong reactions both for and against the proposal. It seems that, on balance, there were more supporters than objectors. With acknowledgements to the company, the following are extracts of letters from both camps:

'I wish to object . . . on the grounds of damage to the environment and the speculative nature of the operation . . . it seems highly doubtful how it could be commercially successful . . . steam trains would bring into a quiet and peaceful part of the countryside noise, smoke and, indeed, sparks. Finally, it is highly doubtful whether the reopening of this line is necessary as a public service. There is already a frequent bus service and there is no reason to duplicate this form of transport.'

Another objector said:

'I wish to object . . . the line divides my property in two and represents a considerable hazard to my employees and stock. The only access to the other half by tractor is across an unmanned level crossing where collisions have only narrowly been avoided in the past in spite of every precaution being taken. Steam trains have an additional fire risk. The use of ratepayers' money on a dubious commercial enterprise of this nature cannot be justified.'

Others, however, expressed different views:

'At a recent meeting . . . a wish to have the railway reopened was unanimously expressed. Study groups would like to visit the depot of the Steam Trust and Company, when ready, in order to see present day and vintage transport in action and in restoration.'

And again:

'I strongly support your application for a Light Railway Order. It will be a great asset to the area to have, once again, a functional railway offering a practical service for shoppers, students and workers travelling to and from Taunton. Not everyone has a car.'

Running alongside the association in those early days was the Minehead Railway Preservation Society, formed in January 1971 by Bryan H. Jackson, a Middlesex publisher. The society's aims were somewhat different from those of the company and association but in the interests of unity, a merger of association and society was agreed. However, differences eventually arose between the two and Mr Jackson resigned from the association with a

Left: Stogumber station viewed towards Bishops Lydeard in the period when the line was closed to all traffic. A group of children makes its way across at the south end of the platform. *Eric Rowlands*

Above: With paint peeling from the wooden platform shelter, Stogumber awaits the return of an operational railway. *Eric Rowlands*

Left: As the weeds grow on both the platform and the trackbed, Crowcombe is pictured before the arrival of Walter Harris and his friends. *Eric Rowlands*

view to reviving the society. The inaugural meeting of the association took place in Taunton on 7 May 1971. The association became and remains the only authorised supporters' organisation.

The working party mentioned above reported in April 1971 and its conclusions, after an intervening quarter of a century, are illuminating.

As is usual in such cases, British Rail required some money 'up front' as a token of the company's bona fides. The sum required was £25,000 but the company was quite unable to raise this sum in the time allowed, so Somerset County Council became involved. The council entered into talks with BR, the outcome of which, to cut a long story short, was that the council would buy the line and lease it back to the company to operate. This was to prove an expensive and almost terminal burden for the company, but more of that anon.

Since there were objections to the granting of a Light Railway Order to the company, a Public Inquiry was scheduled to take place at Taunton on 22 January 1974. However, owing to a late objection by the Western National Bus Co, this was postponed until 2 April. In the event, after negotiations with the bus company, its objection was withdrawn and the way was therefore clear for the Order to be made. However, the granting of a Transfer Order to enable the company to operate trains on behalf of the council, which would own the line, was dependent upon the successful completion of the sale of the line to the council.

In the meantime, although association members had been granted access for some time past to the down side of Taunton station in order to work on the restoration of locomotives and stock which were housed with the Great Western Society's stock, there was as yet no access to the line itself or the stations and buildings.

Readers may be wondering about the contemporary staffing situation. At this time, the company had no paid staff; indeed, it had no staff at all, only officers, and these were extremely few in number. All the preliminary work on the line and rolling stock was done by volunteer members of the association and this was to continue until just before the reopening of the line in March 1976.

The May 1974 newsletter carried momentous news. For those who had waited so long and so patiently, it was announced that the first Permanent Way working party on the line would be held on Saturday 18 May 1974, led by Graham Harwood. This was held at Bishops Lydeard and appears to have been on similar lines to the present-day 'shop till you drop'! It was stressed that access was only for the purposes of WEEDING AND CLEANING UP.

About this time, the company offered the Diesel & Electric Group a home on the line and thus was to begin what has become a mutually most fruitful association.

The very first working party at Minehead station was held on 1 June 1974, also under the able leadership of Graham Harwood. In the meantime, Harry Lee and his band of volunteers were still in Taunton West Yard preparing the steam locomotive *Victor* for the great day when it would pull passenger trains on the revived railway.

September 1974 brought further progress with the granting of the Light Railway Order to the county council.

A noteworthy event took place in March 1975. It was the policy of Butlin's Holiday Camps at certain locations to exhibit static steam locomotives formerly on British Railways. There were two such locomotives at Minehead: No 46229 *Duchess of Hamilton,* an ex-LMS 4-6-2 express passenger locomotive and No 32678 *Knowle* an ex-London, Brighton & South Coast 0-6-0T locomotive of the famous Stroudley 'Terrier' class. In the mid-1970s, Butlin's decided to revoke its policy and consequently the two locomotives had to be moved from the camp. Because of the difficulty of moving the locomotives by road, principally dictated by the railway overbridges, the 'Duchess' in particular either had to be moved by rail or cut up on site.

The company appealed for all available volunteers to assist in cutting back lineside vegetation which had lain undisturbed for over four years, so that a test run could be made by a Class 25 diesel. The vegetation was duly cleared and a successful test run was made on 6 March by No 25225. The 'Duchess' was taken by road to Minehead station, where she was re-railed on what is now the run-round loop. On Thursday 13 March, the 'Duchess' was moved to Taunton by No 25059, being taken to Swindon for overhaul by No D1010 *Western Campaigner* on Monday 17 March.

The 'Terrier' was also re-railed at Minehead, where it spent many years as a static exhibition. It is now on the Kent & East Sussex Railway.

In mid-1975, the Somerset & Dorset Railway Museum Trust requested a home on the line, having been unsuccessful in establishing a base at Radstock. Again, as with the Diesel & Electric Group, this association has been of great mutual benefit, the famous 2-8-0 No 88 (BR No 53808) proving itself an almost indispensable member of the motive power stud.

In the August 1975 Newsletter, it was announced that at last the Light Railway Transfer Order had been granted. It was hoped to operate a service between Minehead and Blue Anchor on Saturdays and Sundays in the latter half of September. However, this was not to be, as the terms of the lease, *inter alia*, were not finalised in time.

At the end of 1975 there occurred serious differences of opinion between the company and the association, mainly due to a lack of communication

of the sort that has happened a number of times over the years but particularly in the early days. As a result, all working parties were suspended until a satisfactory outcome had been achieved. In the event, these differences were resolved and normal relations were resumed at the beginning of 1976.

Sunday 21 December 1975 was a historic day for the fledgeling railway company. That day saw the first train run between Bishops Lydeard and Minehead. This 'Directors' Special' conveyed sundry VIPs, including the local MP, Tom King. It was estimated that some 2,000 people turned out to see the train at Minehead. On this occasion, the driver was Harry Lee, the fireman Roy Hartell and the guard Nick Jones (later to become the railway's first Operating Superintendent). The train consisted of *Victor*, stores van No 150346 and a brake van.

Meanwhile, the company was pressing ahead with the preparations for a share issue which would transform it into a company limited by guarantee. The initial issue was for £65,000. However, such was the enthusiasm that over £90,000 was subscribed before the offer closed. Although a public company, the WSR has never been quoted on the Stock Exchange.

After over five years of extremely hard work, most notably by members of the WSRA, the railway was opened for business on Sunday 28 March 1976. The official opening was performed by Lord Montagu and

over 2,000 passengers were carried on the first day. There were four trains in the timetable, all steam-hauled, departing from Minehead at 10.00, 12.00, 14.00 and 16.00, with a 15min lie-over at Blue Anchor to allow for running round and shunting stock. The timetable, *which is illustrated on page 18,* took the form of flimsy yellow handouts augmented by large posters displayed in prominent places around the locality.

It was in the middle of 1976 that the Taunton branch of the National Union of Railwaymen decided to operate a policy of non-co-operation towards the WSR. The NUR members in question were actually bus drivers, whose allegiance derived from the days when they replaced train drivers on the Taunton–Minehead route. It has been claimed that this alleged attitude by the NUR proved a very useful smokescreen to obscure other incidents over the years.

More unremitting toil resulted in the opening of the line between Blue Anchor and Williton on Saturday 28 August 1976. The route mileage of the line was now some 9¾ miles and the timetable scheduled departure times from Minehead at 09.00, 10.00, 11.15, 12.30, 13.45, 15.00 and 16.15. The day after the March reopening to Blue Anchor, one of the Park Royal diesel multiple-units (DMU) had been brought back into service, so this also shared the

Left: A scene that was typical of many closed railways in the post-Beeching era; dereliction and decay are all too evident in this view of Crowcombe looking south. *Eric Rowlands*

Right: The level crossing gates at Roebuck viewed looking towards Minehead in the period when it seemed that they would be permanently shut to railway traffic. *Eric Rowlands*

Above: A track-level view at Crowcombe looking north illustrates the magnitude of the work required to get the railway operational again. *Eric Rowlands*

Right: The crossing keeper's cottage at Roebuck Crossing. *Eric Rowlands*

Left: With spectacle glass smashed, it seemed as though the Leigh Bridge up distant had cleared its last train. *Eric Rowlands*

Below left: The 1976 timetable.

augmented timetable to Williton to ease the pressure on the modest locomotive fleet. Consequently, of those trains mentioned above, only the 10.00, 12.30 and 15.00 trains were steam-hauled. Departure times from Williton were 09.55, 11.05 (steam), 12.25, 13.35 (steam), 14.55, 16.05 (steam) and 17.25. These punishing schedules with their tight turn-round times were to have dire consequences for the small locomotives which worked the trains, with their limited coal and water capacity.

Despite the buoyant mood throughout the operating season, all was not well with the WSR, and the Directors' Report and Accounts for the six months ended 31 July 1976 was far from encouraging. Serious losses had been incurred even at that point and the decision had been taken to abandon the promised winter service before it had begun. The Annual General Meeting on 30 October 1976 was an acrimonious affair which, despite the proxy votes carrying the day for the board, nevertheless resulted in the entire board resigning and a new one being appointed.

Following much behind-the-scenes activity, the line reopened for a limited winter service with three return trips operating on Tuesdays, Fridays and Saturdays between Minehead and Williton. It was also intended to operate steam specials at Christmas.

1977 saw a severe cut-back of steam services. Although the timetable trumpets 'For this, our second year of operation, the West Somerset Railway is offering over two thousand trains running between 4th April and 9th October', steam worked only as far as Blue Anchor. For those wishing to journey further afield, it was necessary to use the DMUs and only three of these went all the way through during the peak season. On Saturdays, there was no steam at all and this persisted for many years into the future. But at least there were still services of some sort.

In addition to a complicated timetable, not understood by the average traveller, many of whom could not (and still cannot) interpret a BR timetable, an equally complicated system of fares was in operation, necessitating a comprehensive, if not encyclopaedic, knowledge on the part of both booking office clerks and travelling ticket inspectors (TTI). A sample of the 1976 timetable is illustrated here.

Despite the many vicissitudes, there was a little light on the horizon. Southern Television had made a children's programme entitled *The Flockton Flyer*

Steam in Somerset

The West Somerset Railway Company plans to restart train services between Minehead and Taunton later this year.

Meanwhile, limited services drawn by steam locomotives will start between Minehead and Blue Anchor on March 28th. The service will operate on weekdays and Sundays.

Departure times from Minehead:
Daily 10.00, 12.00, 14.00, 16.00. (allowing about 15 minutes in Blue Anchor)

Return fare:
50 pence adult
30 pence child under 14

For further information contact:

THE WEST SOMERSET RAILWAY COMPANY
Railway Station,   16, Elm Grove,
Minehead, TA24 5BG   Taunton, TA1 1EQ
(Tel. 4996)   (Tel. 3339)

Watchet Printing Company, Old Cleeve, Minehead (Washford 513)

on the line the previous year and this was due to be screened in 1977. One of the locomotives, 0-6-0PT No 6412, carried nameplates with the programme's title on it throughout the season and the publicity was responsible for fairly successful commercial results. A second series of the programme was filmed during the year, mainly at Crowcombe Heathfield.

During 1977, the committee of the WSRA authorised the institution of a new West Somerset Railway Journal, to replace the monthly newsletter. This publication, which first appeared in January 1978 and was to be a quarterly magazine, would continue to carry news of both company and association. It was also considered more in keeping with the railway's image as a going concern. Other considerations were that it could carry illustrations and might be sold to the public at the railway's retail outlets.

Other early WSR publications were the *Official Guide Book,* the *Stations and Buildings Book* and the *Stock Review,* the latter first produced by member Tim King in the spring of 1977. Some members were to produce their own contributions such as *Walks from Stogumber Station*, retailing at 5p!

During the latter part of 1976, a start was made on the construction of a pit in the former goods shed (now loco shed) at Minehead. After 6½ months and 1,400 hours of work, the pit was completed, mainly due to the labours of 'Hugh' Perrett, and handed over to the locomotive department on 26 April 1977.

In early February 1978, most of West Somerset was cut off by very severe blizzard conditions affecting the region; the worst, in fact, since the winter of 1962-63. The WSR made strenuous efforts to clear the line in order to re-establish communication with the outside world. The locomotive used was 0-6-0T *Vulcan* in the charge of Harry Lee and it hauled one of the DMU cars. At that time, the line was only open for regular services to Williton and special dispensation was sought and obtained from the Department of Transport for a service to run to Bishops Lydeard.

After numerous attempts to charge through snowdrifts (the WSR has never had snowploughs) on the more exposed sections of line, especially in the Quantock foothills, Bishops Lydeard was finally reached. The train was met by a bus, Post Office van and ambulance from Taunton, together with several private cars containing passengers for the return

Below: One of the first movements after the closure of the line by British Rail was the shipment of the Stanier Pacific No 6229 *Duchess of Hamilton* from the Butlin's holiday camp at Minehead to Taunton for onward movement to the National Railway Museum in March 1975. *Eric Rowlands*

Left: On 28 March 1976, the West Somerset Railway was reopened. On that day Don Spencer is pictured at work in Blue Anchor signalbox. *Eric Rowlands*

Centre left: The two 0-6-0Ts, *Vulcan* and *Victor*, are seen shortly after delivery to Taunton in February 1974. *John Reeves*

Below: On 21 December 1975 a directors' special was run, the first train to be operated by the West Somerset Railway. It is pictured at Williton. *John Reeves*

Below right: Stogumber station pictured in the rain on 19 September 1976. *John Reeves*

train to Minehead. As well as ordinary passengers, the train carried discharged hospital passengers stranded in Taunton, medical supplies and several sacks of Post Office mail, almost certainly the only time Royal Mail has been carried on the line since BR days. This emergency working provided the undignified spectacle of guard Barney Forsdike wearing blue plastic fertiliser sacks tied around his trousers in order to keep out the snow! Fares were improvised, as none had been published for the unopened stretch of line.

The railway held its first Gala Day on Sunday 7 May 1978. Various attractions were on offer, not least a Day Ticket including UNLIMITED TRAVEL for £2 (Adults) and £1.20 (Children under 14)! Another milestone was passed on Gala Day when the line was reopened to Stogumber, a further length of 3½ miles. The lack of run-round facilities meant that only the DMUs could be used on the service.

The July 1978 issue of the journal contained the first constitution the association had ever had. This very necessary document appears to have been entirely overlooked during all the other activity since 1971.

In 1978 the first accommodation coach for volunteers was brought into service at Minehead. There had long been a need for this, and the WSR still lags behind its more progressive competitors in the matter of provision of volunteer accommodation. Wilf Sly and the late Tom Brunskill were responsible for this first coach conversion.

The railway ran its first 'Santa Special' at Christmas 1978. This, it should be noted, did not take the form of the trains of the same name in more recent years; rather, Father Christmas with his attendant fairies and elves travelled from somewhere up the line into Minehead station.

In the April 1979 journal there appeared a loose-leaf advertisement for a special train: 'The Quantock Quest'. This was scheduled to run on Sunday 17

June 1979 and was billed as the first through train since closure of the branch line by BR, as, indeed, it would have been. Sadly, it failed to materialise for one reason or another; just another of the disappointments experienced by those who have worked so long and hard to bring us the splendid railway we enjoy so much today.

Saturday 9 June 1979 was the date set for reopening the remainder of the line for regular passenger services, from Stogumber to Bishops Lydeard. It was decided to hold another Gala Weekend. Although the timetable was far from ambitious, which was just as well in the event, it severely taxed the available steam motive power. So much so, that by the end of the weekend, all the steam had failed, leaving train haulage to No D7017 (the 'Hymek') and the Park Royal DMUs. If nothing else, this vindicated the decision to offer a home on the line to the Diesel & Electric Group.

Notwithstanding the shortcomings in the locomotive department, the weekend was generally reckoned to have been a success. There were many side-shows up and down the line and just about every station put on a display of some sort. Bishops Lydeard boasted a modest display of vintage tractors, engines of the stationary variety and assorted agricultural memorabilia by the South Somerset Agricultural Preservation Club and was the forerunner of the hugely successful WSR Steam Rallies of more recent years held in the field adjoining the station.

It was rapidly becoming apparent that the railway was seriously deficient in suitable steam locomotives for regular and punctual services over such a distance. The two Bagnalls, *Victor* and *Vulcan,* and No 6412 simply did not have the coal and water capacity to pull heavy trains from Minehead to Bishops Lydeard and vice versa without requiring refreshment *en route*. The only proper watering facility was at Minehead, so in 1980 a water tower

(ex-Pwllheli) was erected at Williton. There were to be no satisfactory watering facilities at Bishops Lydeard for some years to come.

Until the arrival of more suitable locomotives, it was necessary to divide the line into two: Minehead–Williton and Williton–Bishops Lydeard. Williton became a sort of frontier station, rather like Beddgelert on the old Welsh Highland and passengers wishing to travel the whole length of the line were obliged to change from the steam train at Williton to a DMU for onward passage to Bishops Lydeard. This had the dual effect of saving wear and tear on the locomotive fleet and enabling a more punctual service to be run. Steam trains did still run to Bishops Lydeard on occasions, but it was the exception rather than the rule.

At this distance in time, it seems quite incredible how slender the motive power resources of the railway actually were. Although there were three regular performers, it was almost unheard of for all three to be available for service simultaneously. More often than not, there was only one and any failure could have disastrous consequences for the timetable!

The years of euphoria were now coming to an end and serious financial problems were looming on the horizon. The summer of 1981 had been, to quote the journal of the WSR, 'nothing short of disastrous for the railway; expenses were too high, passengers too few, morale low and timekeeping appalling'. During the following few years, it was principally the loyalty, devotion and sheer hard work, not to mention injections of substantial sums of cash, by members of the association which kept the line going.

Several times the line had been in imminent peril of closing down, but a lot of faith, more hard work and a further infusion of capital from a share issue in 1983 meant things began to take a turn for the better.

Even in the summer of 1985, there were still only two active steam locomotives on the line running the heavy peak season traffic. These were *Victor* and No 6412. Not until the summer of the following year was the line to see a locomotive which proved the shape of things to come. That year, ex-GWR 2-6-2T No 5572 was hired from the Great Western Society at Didcot to augment the WSR's own fleet. The visit of this locomotive was a great success and from that year on, visiting locomotives were to become a regular feature of the West Somerset's summer timetable.

Another landmark was passed on 28 June 1987, when Doniford Beach Halt was opened. This was an entirely new station and brought the total on the WSR to 10 – more, at that time, than BR had in the whole of Somerset! In August the same year, ex-S&DJR No 88 returned to service, the first new resident WSR locomotive to steam since 1976.

1988 saw ex-GWR 0-6-0 No 3205 move from the Severn Valley to the WSR, where it has been ever since; another valuable addition to the motive power fleet.

The locomotive situation was by now improving in leaps and bounds. However, it may be appropriate here to add a tribute to the Diesel & Electric Preservation Group for unfailing support with their own units. Both the 'Hymek' No D7017 and the Class 14 had proved a godsend on numerous occasions when a combination of factors had proved too much for an ailing steam fleet. Their presence on the railway has been inestimable.

On 23 May 1988, with little ceremony, the last of the Bagnall 0-6-0Ts, *Victor*, left the West Somerset Railway. Despite its many inadequacies and shortcomings on a line of such length and possessing such gradients, *Victor* had been a mainstay of the locomotive stud and its departure was an occasion for not a little nostalgia.

Late in 1988, another share issue was made. This time it was aimed at £500,000 with the principal object being to buy the lease for the line from the county council. Well over £300,000 was raised in the end, enabling the company not only to purchase the lease for 99 years but also to do several other pressing jobs on the line.

Summer 1989 saw the visit of ex-BR No 92220 *Evening Star* to the line for the season; also the return to steam from 'Barry condition' of ex-GWR 2-6-2T No 4561. Nos 6412 and 4561 both belong to the association, which has an agreement for their use with the company. It is of interest that apart from *Victor* and *Vulcan*, the company has not, up to now, owned any other steam locomotives, although it owns most of the coaching stock.

The new Minehead signalbox was commissioned on 12 April 1990. This box began life at Maerdy in South Wales but was subsequently moved to Dunster, where it remained until 1977, when it was moved in one piece by rail to its present location, an operation thought to be unique at the time. The original Minehead box was demolished by BR when the line was 'rationalised' in the 1960s. It stood on the seaward side of the tracks.

There were two historic events for the railway in the summer of 1990. For the first time since

Above right: A view along the platform at Minehead on 5 April 1976 sees, on the left, the ex-Somerset & Dorset Joint 2-8-0 No 53808, the 'Hymek' No 7017 and the two DMU sets, whilst at the front of the goods shed No 6412 is visible. *John Reeves*

Right: No 6412 hauls a five-coach rake of ex-BR Mark 1 coaches on the 16.00 service from Minehead to Blue Anchor near Dunster on 15 April 1976. *John Reeves*

reopening, Bishops Lydeard acquired proper watering facilities with the commissioning of the new water tower. Hitherto, the smaller locomotives in particular had found the 20-mile run somewhat taxing with the only intermediate water facilities being at Williton. The ascent of Crowcombe bank is a hard pull for any locomotive, especially hauling a heavy train on greasy rail.

On 16 June 1990, the first through train to come on to the line from BR since 1971 arrived. This train originated in Manchester and after handing over by BR at the sidings of Taunton Cider at Norton Fitzwarren, Nos 4561 and 6412 double-headed the train to Minehead and back. This train was, happily, the first of many subsequent through excursions.

The West Somerset had begun to recover from the disastrous financial years of the early 1980s and this was evident in new developments all along the line. On 24 March 1991, the line received its first through train from Paddington for over 20 years, whilst in June there were two further noteworthy events to record. On the 10th of the month, the 'Lorna Doone' coach for passengers confined to wheelchairs and their carers was put into service. This vehicle incorporates special anchor points for wheelchairs, separate seats for those accompanying them, special toilet facilities and a hydraulic lift for easy access and exit. The coach is a composite, sharing accommodation with the guard. It is believed to be the only vehicle of its type running anywhere in the British Isles at the time of writing. At the end of that month, the Visitor Centre at Bishops Lydeard was

opened by actor and author Bill Pertwee, well known for his appearances in, amongst other things, the legendary television situation comedy *Dad's Army*.

Early 1992 witnessed the construction of a new booking office at Bishops Lydeard and the start of work on the new shed (ex-Swindon) at Williton. There had long been a need for both these facilities; the layout at Bishops Lydeard simply did not lend itself to the speedy turn-round of trains using the old booking office located in the station building, while covered accommodation for restoration and maintenance of stock was not only at a premium but barely existed at all! Most work on locomotives and stock had been carried out al-fresco since 1976 and even before.

1992 marked the 150th year since the entry of the railway to Taunton and it was decided that some suitable celebration would be in order, so an event based loosely on Darlington 150 was organised to be centred on Bishops Lydeard. Fortuitously, the legendary GWR locomotive *City of Truro* was to visit the line during the summer, so the event was tailored to suit this visit. Sundry other visiting locomotives also appeared but undoubtedly the star attraction was the record-breaking *City of Truro*. As part of the celebrations, BR agreed to stable Collett 0-6-0 No 3205 in the down bay platform at Taunton. This attracted considerable attention and there were tales of BR drivers alighting from their HST cabs to try No 3205's footplate for size with much nostalgia all round!

Taunton 150 was an unqualified success and has

been followed in subsequent years by other celebrations of historical events. 1994, for instance, was marked by a special weekend celebration of the 50th year since D-Day.

A new locomotive stabling compound with pit was constructed just south of Bishops Lydeard station. There is also accommodation for train crews and this provides long-needed security for motive power during the summer season when the all-steam service operates.

In the autumn of that year, several remarkable events took place. The new shed at Williton was handed over by Tarmac, who had generously donated the building, moved it from Swindon and erected it on site, on 25 September. On 3 October, the railway ran the longest and heaviest passenger train ever seen on a preserved line: 19 coaches (767½ tons) pulled by ex-GWR 2-8-0 No 3822, the season's visiting engine. The idea was to run non-stop from Minehead to Bishops Lydeard but weather conditions conspired to defeat the non-stop element of this gallant attempt. However, despite the dark and rain, many people turned out all along the line to cheer on the locomotive crew.

Hard on the heels of this marathon, the West Somerset held its first 'Friends of Thomas the Tank Engine' weekend on 24/25 October. These events had been held on other lines for quite a number of years but the WSR was slow to follow. The idea of locomotives with faces painted on did not appeal greatly to some traditionalists, but financial realities prevailed in the end. Despite it being right at the end

of the season and pretty chilly to boot, the event was obviously a success and several such weekends have been held since, seeming to improve as staff gain experience. With a line the length of the WSR, running the extra trains these occasions demand entails much detailed planning to integrate the extra short workings to Blue Anchor and back with the regular service. Indeed, if electric key token working (see section on Train Working) had not been introduced between Minehead and Blue Anchor, such extra services would probably not be possible.

The pilot driver training course for enthusiasts was run in November and on 5 December the restored loop at Crowcombe Heathfield was used for the first time, when No 3205 ran round a 'Santa Special'.

The original aim of the company was the restoration of a railway link with Taunton and the running of regular commuter and shopping trains. While no longer company policy in the short or medium term, the matter is still aired frequently by many people and it can be an emotive subject. It is probably true to say that it is the ambition of everyone connected with the line to see this goal achieved, but all the realists appreciate that such a goal must not be at the expense of destroying the tremendous amount that has been achieved. The capital costs, at the time of writing, mean that such a project is just not viable, although ways to get round the difficulties are constantly being explored.

In 1993, the company commissioned a study on

Left: During the first week of January 1979 steam provided the motive power for the daily trains. *Vulcan* heads the 12.30 Minehead-Stogumber service between Williton and its destination. The train is formed of a DMU trailer car and a BGZ stove van. *Stephen Edge*

Below left: The first public train over the Bishops Lydeard-Norton Fitzwarren section was a DMU special chartered by the Branch Line Society in 1980. It is seen passing Tone Vale Bridge. *Stephen Edge*

Above right: One of the most unusual vehicles to operate over the West Somerset Railway is this road-rail bus converted from a Bristol LH. It is seen at Bishops Lydeard in August 1980 being eased back on to terra firma. *Stephen Edge*

Centre right: During the lean years of the early 1980s, the railway took any traffic on offer, as is witnessed in this scene of a temporarily converted ex-BR Mark 1 BSK No 25357 being unloaded at Bishops Lydeard in October 1982. Guard John Guest looks on. *John Glover*

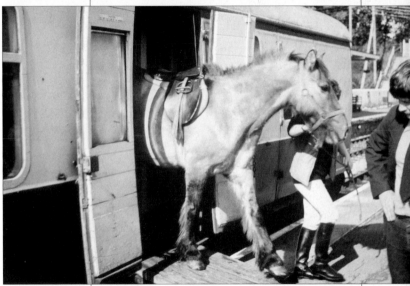

Below: Unfortunately, the two 0-6-0Ts, *Vulcan* and *Victor*, proved too small for operation and have now left the railway. On 23 May 1988 the latter lets off steam for the last time on the WSR as it awaits the low-loader at Bishops Lydeard. *Peter Thompson*

Above left:
No 4561 brings an empty coaching stock working into Williton on 5 October 1989. This was the locomotive's first trial run after restoration to working order. *Peter Thompson*

Left: On 14 October 1989 the up special crosses the down DMU at Williton. *Peter Thompson*

Above: The ex-S&DJR 2-8-0 No 53808 approaches Roebuck Gate Crossing on 5 August 1989 with the 12.30 from Minehead to Bishops Lydeard service. Normally a DMU turn, it was steam operated on this occasion to Bishops Lydeard so that the locomotive could operate the evening 'Starlight Express'. *Stephen Edge*

the development of the line including, amongst other matters, the implications of through running to Taunton. This is an interesting and thoughtful document, which outlines clearly the costs and possible consequences of through running. Other alternatives were explored, including the replacement of a station at Norton Fitzwarren for the direct exchange of passengers to and from the main line and bringing trains from the main line as far as Bishops Lydeard or even to Minehead. The

latter option is now actively being pursued and, of course, charter trains come on to the line from all parts of the country on a regular basis.

The report containing the conclusions of this study can be obtained upon payment from the company headquarters at Minehead station.

1993 appears to have produced fewer occasions of note than the previous year. However, there were two events worth recounting. The first was on 30 April, when the railway ran its first charter freight for photographers. Again, the WSR was later in this field than some others, but this first venture was a great success and has led to more in succeeding years.

The line from Norton Fitzwarren to Bishops Lydeard had been passed some time previously by BR for its locomotives and stock to traverse the section. On 16 June 1993, the first InterCity 125 set came on to the branch as far as Bishops Lydeard on a charter working, the passengers transferring to a WSR steam-hauled train for onward passage to Minehead.

As previously mentioned, the 50th anniversary of D-Day fell in 1994 and it was decided to put on a 'Wartime Weekend' to commemorate the major part played by the railways and their staffs during World War 2. This event took place on 7/8 May and was a great success due to a great deal of hard work put in by the usual small band of dedicated organisers.

Among the attractions offered were special military freight trains carrying contemporary tanks and other military vehicles, which their owners had brought to the line especially for the occasion.

Just prior to this event, on 27 April, the first through working from BR to be steam-hauled for 30 years took place. This train originated on the Severn Valley Railway at Kidderminster and the object of the exercise was to bring down BR Standard Class 4 No 75069 from the SVR to the WSR, where it was to spend the summer season.

Following considerable efforts, the loop at Crowcombe Heathfield was commissioned on 10 May. That day, the railway was visited by Major John Poyntz, recently appointed to HM Railway Inspectorate, who took the opportunity to inspect the entire line after he had passed the loop for passenger working. At present, the loop is used only for crossing trains run in connection with special or very intensive timetables, but it adds immeasurably to the line's flexibility when late running occurs and it is a desperately needed addition to the line's facilities.

1994 turned out to be a record year for the West Somerset, with over 127,000 passengers being carried: an all-time high up to then. Yet another historical milestone was reached on 23 September, when the West Somerset Railway Association became a company limited by guarantee.

A further issue of shares was made in 1994, with some £100,000 being raised by the end of September 1995.

1995 proved again a most successful year with a

Left: 'Hymek' No 7017 is pictured by the sea at Helwell Bay, near Watchet, bound for Williton with the 12.20 service from Minehead on 7 May 1978. *Stephen Edge*

Below left: The two-car Gloucester-built DMU approaches Bishops Lydeard on 23 April 1988 with the 10.10 service from Minehead. *Stephen Edge*

Above right: Pictured at Crowcombe Bridge, the ex-S&DJR 2-8-0 No 53808 passes with the 16.00 Minehead-Bishops Lydeard service on 30 May 1988. *Stephen Edge*

Right: With Watchet harbour in the background, a suitably begrimed No 53808 pulls away from the station on 2 September 1990. *Dave Taylor*

number of noteworthy events to record. Apart from all the regular events, such as the Gala Weekends, there was a Victory Weekend on 1/2 July to celebrate the 50th anniversary of the end of the war. Special trains, both passenger and goods, (including a train carrying military vehicles) were run. The second 'Friends of Thomas the Tank Engine' Weekend (21/22 October) broke all records, with passenger figures 27% up on the October 1994 event and even a 10% increase over the July 1995 weekend!

One piece of good news with far-reaching implications for the line was the raising of the axle-loading limit to 23.5 tonnes. This means the railway can accept the heaviest steam and diesel locomotives likely to be available.

When this book closed for press, work was proceeding apace on the facilities at Williton and the new machine shop at Minehead. By the time this book is published, it is hoped that work will have been completed on lengthening the loop at Bishops Lydeard and a start will have been made on the platform extension and permanent shop there.

It is heartening to record that the season ended on a most positive and upbeat note. As at the end of October 1995, passenger figures were approximately 4% up compared with the same date in 1994 — 121,155 and 116,792 respectively. Revenue showed an increase of approximately 6½%. Since the passenger figure total for the end of 1994 was 127,177, there is every confidence that this year's total will show a comfortable increase.

Such welcome news can only be reassuring for those who rely on the railway for a livelihood, for the shareholders, for all those volunteers who put so much into the project and, not by any means least, all those visitors who so much enjoy what our line has to offer. We can surely face our second quarter-century in a spirit of considerable optimism.

Below left: Hauled by ex-GWR 2-6-2T No 4561, the 1990 Shareholders' Special departs from Washford. *Peter Thompson*

Bottom left: On 14 May 1991 ex-GWR 2-6-2T No 4561 receives a bunkerful of coal prior to leaving the shed at Minehead for a day's work on the line. The grounded boiler beyond the locomotive is from the ex-GWR 2-8-0 No 3850. *Stephen Edge*

Above right: The first visit of a Class 37 to the line occurred on 1 November 1992. The locomotive, No 37699, is seen approaching Doniford Beach Halt. *Peter Thompson*

Right: A dream of the future? Collett-designed 0-6-0 No 3205 is seen in the bay platform at Taunton in 1992. *John Pearce*

Below: Some 'Friends of Thomas the Tank Engine' are caught on camera on 13 June 1993. *Brian Smith*

Above: Ex-GWR 0-6-0 No 3205 brings the 10.25 Bishops Lydeard-Minehead train into Watchet on 2 September 1992. This scene is now but a memory for just three months later, in January 1993, Watchet harbour closed to commercial shipping, ending a tradition that stretched back for many generations. *Stephen Edge*

Centre left: Through trains return: HST power car No 43102 and ex-GWR 0-6-0 No 3205 are seen side-by-side at Taunton in 1992. A fine study! *Courtesy Editor* WSR Journal

Below left: Class 37 No 37699 makes an impressive sight as it enters Blue Anchor on 1 November 1992 with a service from Minehead to Bishops Lydeard. *Stephen Edge*

Right: On 30 May 1992 ex-GWR 2-8-0 No 3822 is pictured departing from Watchet with the 12.15 Bishops Lydeard-Minehead train. *Stephen Edge*

Above: On 10 August 1992 GWR 2-8-0 No 3822 heads the 15.55 Bishops Lydeard-Minehead across Woolston Moor towards Cottisford Bridge. *Stephen Edge*

Left: A dramatic view of ex-GWR 2-8-0 No 3822 heading the 14.10 to Minehead from Bishops Lydeard on 2 May 1992. *Stephen Edge*

Above right: On 16 January 1993 the first HST excursion traversed the WSR. It is seen at Norton Fitzwarren junction heading towards Bishops Lydeard. It originated at Bedford. *Stephen Edge*

Right: On 5 June 1993 the first through train to originate from the WSR for 22 years departed from Minehead to York. It was hauled over the WSR by ex-LMS Class 8F No 48773 and from Bishops Lydeard motive power was provided by three Class 50s: Nos 50033, D400 and 50007 *Sir Edward Elgar.* The 12-coach train approaches the junction at Norton Fitzwarren. *Stephen Edge*

Above: An unfamiliar locomotive on the WSR: ex-LMS Class 8F 2-8-0 No 48773 came to the line on loan in 1993. On 18 September 1993 it hauled a return special from Minehead to Walsall over the line. *Stephen Edge*

Left: How we like to see it! The crowds at Bishops Lydeard seen on 18 September 1993. *Peter Thompson*

Above right: History is made on 6 March 1995 as BR Class 33 No 33116 stands at Minehead station with the 16.25 return working to London Waterloo. The earlier down working had brought the first working of a 'Crompton' to the line. *Stephen Edge*

Above: BR Standard 4-6-0 No 75069 works a Bishops Lydeard-Minehead train at Nethercott on 30 April 1994. *Stephen Edge*

Right: Crowcombe Heathfield pictured on 29 May 1995. The 14.50 from Minehead crosses the 16.00 from Bishops Lydeard. Note the steep gradient into the station visible from the coaching stock behind No 7828 *Odney Manor*. *Peter Thompson*

Left: Driver Dave Bosley checks his train as No 4160 pulls away from the water tank at Bishops Lydeard with a re-created wartime freight on 7 May 1994. *Peter Thompson*

Below left: Santa waves goodbye to his visitors as a Santa Train departs from Crowcombe for Bishops Lydeard on 8 December 1990. *Stephen Edge*

Above: Class 9F No 92220 *Evening Star* arrives at Bishops Lydeard with a train from Minehead. *John Reeves*

Right: 'Hymek' diesel-hydraulic No D7017 approaches Blue Anchor with a short train. *Stephen Edge*

Below: Steam power on the saw bench at the WSRA rally held at Bishops Lydeard annually in August. Dave Williams is on the engine. As well as being Rally Steam Steward, Dave is also a volunteer driver on the WSR. *Courtesy Editor* WSR Journal

Left: Bishops Lydeard station pictured on 7 March 1976, looking north. The locomotives are Nos 4561, 5542 and 5521 which are all awaiting restoration. Compare this view of 20 years ago with that of today. *John Reeves*

Below left: 'Hymek' No D7017 passes Roebuck Gate Crossing with a special from Minehead. *Bob Tiller*

Above: Before reopening, *Victor* shunts ex-GWR camping coaches at Minehead c1976. At that time stock moves from the main line to the bay platforms required a trip to Dunster! *Courtesy Editor* WSR Journal

Above right: A VIP visit in 1989. Standing in front of No 92220 *Evening Star* are (left to right) the late Robert Adley MP, the Rt Hon Tom King MP, David Nicholson MP and The Hon Bill McAlpine. They are accompanied on the extreme right by guard Bert Blake, who is now the stationmaster at Minehead. *Norman Hawkes*

Right: The lamp room at Williton. *Peter Thompson*

Left: No 4561 brings a train from Minehead into Williton on 1 January 1991. This scene has now changed beyond recognition. *Peter Thompson*

Below left: Locomotion at Bishops Lydeard during the Taunton 150 celebrations on 5 July 1992. Trevor Barnett (on the tender, in overalls) keeps a professional eye on the proceedings. *Stephen Edge*

Bottom: A good trailing load for ex-GWR 0-6-0PT No 6412 at Nethercott, between Bishops Lydeard and Crowcombe Heathfield, on the 11.50 service from Bishops Lydeard on 1 January 1992. *Stephen Edge*

Above right: A fine night shot of the Cravens-built two-car DMU in platform 2 at Minehead on 31 October 1992. *Stephen Edge*

Right: In the evening gloom of 1 January 1993 ex-GWR 0-6-0 No 3205 prepares to depart from Bishops Lydeard with the 16.40 service to Minehead. *Stephen Edge*

Above: This scene might be 30 years earlier than July 1994, when the photograph was actually taken. The train is the 14.40 from Bishops Lydeard to Minehead and is pictured at Crowcombe Heathfield. *Stephen Edge*

Left: The 'Quantock Explorer' HST special from Bedford passes the ornamental grounds of Dene Court to Bishops Lydeard on 30 April 1994. *Stephen Edge*

Top right: Against a backdrop of the Welsh mountains and the Bristol Channel, 0-4-0ST *Kilmersdon* brings a short goods from Minehead into Blue Anchor on 8 May 1994. *Peter Thompson*

Centre right: On 29 April 1994 Peckett 0-4-0ST *Kilmersdon* passes Blue Anchor with a re-created trip freight working from Washford to Minehead. *Stephen Edge*

Right: Hauled by ex-S&DJR 2-8-0 No 88 (53808), the 'Clear up' train calls at Williton *en route* to Bishops Lydeard on 5 March 1994. *Peter Thompson*

Above: Resplendent in its Railfreight livery, Class 50 No 50149 *Defiance* double-heads the 17.45 Bishops Lydeard-Minehead train into Crowcombe Heathfield on 17 April 1995 with ex-S&DJR 2-8-0 No 88. *Stephen Edge*

Below: On 17 June 1995 the unique BR Standard Pacific No 71000 *Duke of Gloucester* stands in the goods shed road at Bishops Lydeard. The locomotive had arrived from Goodrington Sidings the previous day. *Stephen Edge*

Stations and Buildings

The company was most fortunate to inherit all surviving stations and buildings, throughout the whole length of the line, relatively intact. There are some notable examples of both Bristol & Exeter and Great Western architecture, Williton being worthy of mention as one of the former. Several buildings have listed status and these will be described in due course.

Since the line is worked from Minehead, the stations will be described travelling back towards Taunton. From early photographs of the station, Minehead appears to have been a terminus of very modest dimensions. It was opened on 16 July 1874, upon completion of the extension from Watchet. As a matter of interest, this extension was called the West Somerset Railway. The station was enlarged several times and whilst it undoubtedly fulfilled its function as a terminus satisfactorily in former days, its somewhat cramped situation can have serious shortcomings when large crowds are about.

The present company has never had a waiting room at Minehead, although it has to be said that there is really little need for one. In 1976, the former parcels office was converted into a shop and buffet. The latter was adequate during quiet periods but could become congested at busy times and it was not possible to provide the kind of fast service required. Consequently, the buffet was phased out and the shop extended to its present dimensions, while refreshments have since been provided in a coach stabled at the end of the shed road, adjacent to the promenade.

The company has its offices at Minehead station. However, developments over the years have meant

Below: On 26 August 1994 'Manor' class 4-6-0 No 7802 *Bradley Manor* prepares to depart from Minehead with the 10.15 service to Bishops Lydeard. *Stephen Edge*

Above: Hauled by two Class 14 diesel-hydraulics a train arrives at Blue Anchor during a Diesel Gala Weekend. *Peter Barnfield*

Left: Washford station captured in the era before the Somerset & Dorset Railway Trust arrived at this near-derelict station in the mid-1970s. *Eric Rowlands*

Right: Dereliction at Watchet; notice the locals using the line as a footpath. *Eric Rowlands*

that a portable office has had to be located at the rear of the building to provide more office space.

The present locomotive shed was originally the goods shed. Over the years, it has had a pit installed, while coaling, watering and other facilities have been added. The turntable at present visible in the yard will be installed as time and funds permit. Considering the relatively primitive facilities available, miracles of engineering are performed at Minehead Loco! Plans are in hand to extend the shed in order to provide more much-needed covered accommodation.

The signalbox at the east end of the station began life at Maerdy in South Wales. It was subsequently moved to Dunster to control the double line section from there to Minehead. In 1977, it was moved in one piece by rail to Minehead, where it replaced Minehead

Ground Frame, which controlled entry to and exit from main and bay platforms for many years.

Dunster station, likewise, was opened in 1874. Normally, a place such as Dunster would not have merited such a grand station building but, of course, it served Dunster Castle and was the point of arrival for guests at the castle, among whom were Indian potentates arriving to play polo on the lawn beneath the castle. The goods yard saw a good deal of horse-box traffic carrying polo ponies right up to 1939 and the outbreak of World War 2. The station building itself was used by Hornby as the basis for its Dublo branch-line station. The goods shed is listed Grade II and is now used as the depot for the Permanent Way Department.

Blue Anchor, the next station, was also opened in 1874. This is the first passing loop from Minehead and was the terminus of the line from March to August 1976. There was a siding here where the three camping coaches now stand, but the point was removed before reopening for use at Minehead. This point was jacked up and run down to Minehead by hand on two trolleys! As with every other station on the line, everything has been completely refurbished since 1976. The level crossing is the only one left in the West of England which is controlled by a wheel in the signalbox. The former waiting room on the down side (the platform for Minehead) was used as a shop initially but is now a splendid museum run by the West Somerset Steam Railway Trust and devoted mainly to exhibits from the former Great Western Railway. It is an essential place to visit when on the line.

To the west of the level crossing is a small lamp room built of corrugated iron. These were commonplace on the railways when all signal lamps were illuminated by oil lamps, as are many signal lamps on the West Somerset today and these buildings are still used for their original purpose.

The next stop is Washford, at the summit of a two-mile bank, the steepest part of which is 1 in 65. The station is situated on the edge of the village, adjacent to the main A39 and is now the home of the Somerset & Dorset Railway Trust. A 'greenfield' site in March 1976, this station has been transformed by the dedication and hard work of SDRT members.

There is an interesting museum in the station building relating to the former S&D and the small cabin on the platform has been re-created as Midford signalbox. It is possible to go inside and operate the lever frame. The original Bristol & Exeter Railway nameboard survives here, facing the main road. Washford was reopened by the present company on 28 August 1976.

Going on up the line we reach Watchet. This was once the principal source of goods traffic on the line and was originally opened on 31 March 1862 as the then terminus of the line. Watchet harbour was a busy port and had been since medieval times; in order to tap the traffic on offer, extensive sidings were constructed in the broad gauge (7ft 0¼in) to which the line was built, down to the quayside. There was also a siding to the paper mill. Goods traffic ceased on 6 July 1964 and the lines were lifted shortly afterwards. The only evidence remaining that such facilities ever existed is the old goods shed on the town side of the line.

The station and ancillary buildings are unchanged from the date of reopening in 1976 but, of course, there has been extensive refurbishment, as everywhere else. It is the busiest intermediate station on the railway and is the only one which is situated in the middle of the place it purports to serve. It was reopened by the present company on 28 August 1976.

The first new station to be opened on the railway is

Left: Another demonstration freight, this time hauled by ex-GWR 2-6-2T No 6106 passes Doniford Beach Halt on 5 September 1991. *Stephen Edge*

moved it from its original home at the former Swindon locomotive works and erected it on its present site. Two roads run through the shed and with its attendant sidings, it is used for the restoration and maintenance of both locomotives and rolling stock. It is a most valuable addition to the line, where covered facilities have been almost non-existent until recent years.

Plans are in hand here to construct a new two-road shed adjacent to the goods shed as covered accommodation for diesel locomotives, where volunteers can work on them protected from the elements.

Three miles from Williton lies Stogumber station. Like one or two other stations on the line, it is fairly remote from the place whose name it carries, being about a mile from the village of the same name. It was reopened by the present company on 7 May 1978. Owing to there being no run-round loop here, the service could only be run using DMU stock. Nevertheless, it was another small step to reopening the whole line.

The station building has not altered externally since 1976; however, the platform and waiting facilities have both changed somewhat. The platform inherited from BR was constructed of sleepers, in a fashion typical of a Great Western halt. It had the luxury of a wooden shelter, which has been isolated since the demolition of the rotten sleeper platform. The existing platform has been constructed under the auspices of the present company, as has the new shelter, the majority of the work being carried out by volunteer members of The Friends of Stogumber Station. It is intended eventually to reinstate the platform to its original length.

A camping coach once stood in the yard at Stogumber and this facility has been reinstated recently, although not in precisely the same position as its predecessor.

Going on towards Taunton, the next station encountered is Crowcombe Heathfield. Just under three miles from Stogumber, it is reached after climbing to the summit of the line up a bank, the steepest gradient of which is a short section of 1 in 62, but mainly 1 in 92. This bank is a severe test of a locomotive with a heavy train and could be the cause of major difficulty for the small locomotives used after reopening to Bishops Lydeard in 1979.

Crowcombe Heathfield station was opened originally on 31 March 1862. In December 1889, the 'Heathfield' was dropped to avoid confusion with Heathfield near Newton Abbot. Just over 100 years

Doniford Beach Halt, between Watchet and Williton. This was officially opened on 6 May 1988 but closed soon afterwards, owing to difficulties with access. These difficulties have now been resolved and the Halt is again in full use. However, it is not used for winter services.

Williton is the principal intermediate station on the line and another passing loop. Although the station building here is unchanged since reopening on 28 August 1976, the station environs have changed considerably since that date. It is the only station on the railway as a complete entity to have its building, goods shed and signalbox listed Grade II. This is primarily due to it being the last surviving working example of a Bristol & Exeter Railway station.

As inherited in 1971, the company took over the basic passing facility and a siding into the goods shed. Very early on, the goods shed and siding were assigned to the Diesel & Electric Preservation Group and they are there to this day, Williton being the railway's diesel depot. Since the DEPG took over, a further siding has been laid in roughly where the line to the (now demolished) cattle dock once ran.

The most radical development at Williton has been the advent of the 'Swindon Shed'. This is another listed building and was given to the railway by Tarmac (Swindon) Ltd, who also most generously

later, for the 1991 season, the 'Heathfield' was
restored after complaints from passengers that the
name Crowcombe was misleading, the station being
about 2½ miles from the village! The Victorians were
made of sterner stuff and thought little of walking
five miles or even more to a railway station!

This is the third passing loop from Minehead,
although due to lack of finance and resources, it was
not reinstated by the present company until 1994,
the down loop (the Minehead platform) being used as
a siding until then. In 1971, Crowcombe had been
reduced to an unstaffed halt, like most other stations
on the line. The signalbox had long since been
demolished and the points clipped for through
running. Since 1971, the loop has been reinstated,
the necessary signalling and pointwork installed and
the new signalbox built from scratch, largely with
volunteer labour. Together with the loving
restoration of the remainder of the station and its
surroundings, it is a superb example of a Great
Western country station and reflects considerable
credit upon all those involved.

There now follows the descent down Crowcombe
bank to Bishops Lydeard in the Vale of Taunton
Deane, a distance of about four miles. Bishops
Lydeard is the southern terminus of the line for all
practical purposes. Again, the layout here has altered
since reopening and more alterations are scheduled.
As inherited from BR in 1971, there was a simple
passing loop and a siding into the goods shed. This
siding was unusual in that it had a single slip point
off the down line, the only example of a slip point on
the line. The Department of Transport Inspector (as
he was then) did not much care for this arrangement
and the slip was removed before reopening by the
present company.

Because the line was reopened from the Minehead
end, the majority of the passengers came from there
for many years. However, in more recent times, a
much larger number of passengers start their
journeys at Bishops Lydeard. It has therefore been
necessary for this station to undergo something of a
radical transformation from a sleepy wayside station
to a busy terminus. The staff, too, have had to adapt
to a completely different ethos. Today, this station is
smart, well-kept and staffed in a highly professional
manner, while seeing passengers in numbers that
can only have been dreamt of by the original
promoters of the line.

In 1971, there were two platforms, a station
building on the down side and a small wooden
shelter on the up side. The dereliction was
considerable, not assisted by the destructive
attentions of bored residents of an adjacent housing
estate – a problem that has not entirely disappeared
even after 25 years of occupation!

In the early years, the Taunton Model Railway
Group made themselves a home on the down

Above: Atmosphere at Williton: the restored vintage ticket
office viewed in September 1992. *Stephen Edge*

platform in a well-camouflaged corrugated-iron hut
between the goods shed and the station building. The
goods shed, at first used for storing waste paper
collected to raise funds for the railway, later became
a workshop for rolling stock restoration. It is now a
Visitor Centre containing a lecture room, an
exhibition hall and a model railway. It is open at
most times when trains are operating.

The signalbox has been restored with a 33-lever
frame and will be recommissioned when the station
layout is revised in the not-too-distant future. It was
decommissioned by British Railways on 1 March
1970. Most of the old up line leading from the station
towards Taunton has been lifted but a headshunt
remains. Just south of the station a locomotive
stabling point has been constructed in recent years.
This is used for the steam locomotives running the
summer service. Passenger car parking was once an
embarrassment, but has now been partially solved by
buying the lease on the present car park on the up
side of the station. Eventually, a new car park is to be
constructed in the field adjacent to the present car
park.

With trains arriving at and leaving from the up platform, considerable difficulties could arise both for passengers and staff when the old ticket office in the station building was in use. The safety of passengers and the general public is of paramount importance and with the ever-increasing traffic, it was essential to reduce the number of pedestrians using the barrow crossing at the north end of the station. At the end of June 1992, a brand-new two-window custom-built wooden booking office was opened at the south end of the up platform, thus passengers park their cars and walk straight through the turnstile and on to the trains. This facility has greatly assisted both train and station staff in getting trains away on time, with marked improvements to train running.

Bishops Lydeard station and the adjacent fields are the venue for the perennially popular WSR Steam Rally, which is held on the first weekend in August. This rally has now become one of the 'musts' on the West Country calendar, attracting hundreds of exhibits and thousands of visitors every year.

Below: Visiting ex-GWR 2-6-2T No 5572 arrives at Crowcombe on a train from Minehead. *John Reeves*

Bottom: The line has featured many times on film and television. Here a scene from the BBC's *Miss Marple* is being shot at Bishops Lydeard during 1992. *Courtesy Editor* WSR Journal

Permanent Way

The permanent way consists of the rails, sleepers, ballast and ground upon which the railway runs. The West Somerset Railway Co is responsible for just over 22½ miles of line between Norton Fitzwarren and Minehead, together with most bridges, culverts and 45 miles of fencing.

With the exception of the Festiniog and its newly-acquired Welsh Highland Railway mileage, ours is the longest 'preserved' railway in the country and certainly the longest standard gauge line presently operating. Responsibility for maintenance of the line is divided between the company and the association, an arrangement which helps to keep down costs. The company takes responsibility for the line between Minehead and Williton, while the association looks after things between Williton and Norton Fitzwarren. The dividing line is on the Taunton side of the level-crossing at Williton.

The line has to be walked regularly, to check that all is in order and that there are no broken rail ends, loose fishplates (which join one rail to another), no missing keys (securing rails to chairs on sleepers), no broken chairs and to see which sleepers require replacing.

Much of the WSR has always been wooden sleepers and steam locomotives are not kind to these, tending to set them on fire with dropped coals, which can quickly burn through the creosoted wood. Station staff often have to sally forth with buckets of water during the summer to quench sleeper fires before they get out of hand, with more serious and less accessible outbreaks having to be dealt with by the local fire brigades. The line is now steadily being relaid with concrete sleepers, which last longer, do not catch fire and can be tamped mechanically.

Until very recently, all track maintenance has been carried out by hand and much credit is due to those who carry out this hard work. Machinery is now hired from time to time, particularly out of season, to ease the burden and speed up the work.

Below: Work on the railway: in June 1974 progress is in hand at Crowcombe station clearing the vegetation. *John Reeves*

Lineside vegetation is another aspect of permanent way maintenance which has to be kept constantly under review. A trip on the line will swiftly reveal what a lot has to be controlled and having been done by hand for many years (some of it still is), a rail-mounted flail is now used to augment the efforts of the manual workers.

In this environmentally conscious age, due attention must be paid to conservation, since railway embankments and cuttings are well-known haunts of rare flora and fauna. However, something else which needs careful monitoring is the damage done by rabbits burrowing into cuttings and embankments. This tends to be a problem around Crowcombe Heathfield and culls are regularly carried out, otherwise dangerous landslips might occur, especially in the winter when the weather is inclement.

Although the main line remains the same as it was in 1971, some alterations have, perhaps inevitably, been made to siding accommodation. After reopening, the rails were gradually lifted by the present company from the up side between Minehead and Dunster and between Bishops Lydeard and Norton Fitzwarren. The rails have been used elsewhere. Other alterations at intermediate stations include removal of the point into the siding at Blue Anchor, extensive track relaying at Washford by the Somerset & Dorset Railway Trust, installation of extensive sidings at Williton in connection with the new 'Swindon' shed, removal of the point and siding at Crowcombe Heathfield and major modifications to

the layout at Bishops Lydeard to make it easier to work as a terminal station.

After closure in 1971, Dunster had no sidings, these having been removed subsequent to cessation of goods services. Since reopening, the siding through the shed has been reinstated in connection with, amongst other things, the establishment of the Permanent Way Depot at Dunster. It is possible that further sidings may be laid in here in due course.

The layout at Minehead has, perforce, changed dramatically since 1971. Upon closure, the double track from Dunster remained *in situ*. However, upon takeover by the present company, the layout at Minehead station consisted simply of two roads each side of the island platform. There were no run-round facilities and the platform 1 road terminated well short of the railings on the promenade. Prior to reopening in March 1976, the platform 1 road was extended to the present buffer stops, a run-round loop was reinstated and a siding through the shed was installed. Some minor alterations were made during the intervening years, but it was with the installation of the level-crossing over Seaward Way that the most radical alterations took place, resulting in the comprehensive layout we see today.

Indeed, minor alterations to the yard are ongoing, as requirements change. A long-term aim is to reinstate the turntable when resources permit, although it is thought that this will be done on the landward side of the station, using land made available by the council.

Far left: The association Permanent Way gang installs the loop at Crowcombe Heathfield on 8 December 1991. The team is led by Dave Randall, who is furthest from the camera. *Stephen Edge*

Left: Just to show that the staff do not go to Spain for six months in the winter. Steve Martin (Operating Superintendent, left) and Dave Bosley (Running Shed Foreman) tackle the waterproofing on the bridge at Stogumber. *Cedric Dunmall*

Above right: The Permanent Way Department do some spot resleepering — an often forgotten aspect of what running a railway is all about! *Norman Hawkes*

Centre right: Pat Langan (front) and Ian Jonas demonstrate the 'instant turntable' on 1 November 1993. They seem a little apprehensive! *Peter Thompson*

Below right: Work on the railway: the run-round loop at Minehead station is relaid during the winter of 1975-76. *Eric Rowlands*

Train Working

Like most branch lines, the West Somerset Railway is single track. This means that for the majority of its length, the trains run in both directions over the same line of rails. This form of working, of course, is potentially most hazardous unless certain well-defined rules are laid down and this has been recognised since the very first days of railways as public passenger carriers.

There are a number of ways in which safe working can be maintained on single lines of railway, some of which may be familiar to readers. The most basic is 'One Engine in Steam' (OES), sometimes also described as 'One Train Working' (OTW). This means just what it says: only one train may occupy a specified length of railway at any time.

The next rung up the ladder is 'Train Staff and Ticket' working. For this, a staff is provided for each section. It is usually made of wood and has a characteristic shape and colour for a particular section, so that it is instantly recognisable. The train staff is the train driver's authority to proceed into the section to which

it relates and he may not proceed without it, except in certain rare and well-defined circumstances.

Because the 'Train Staff' system is recognised as being inflexible, in other words trains must alternate in a strictly 'one up, one down' sequence, the 'Ticket' was devised. Tickets are numbered sequentially and contained in a book, which is kept in a box to which access is obtained by a key on the end of the train staff. This box is normally kept in the signalbox.

If two or more trains are to pass in the same direction before a return train is scheduled, the signalman will issue a ticket to the train driver, first showing him the staff relating to the section and thus proving that no preceding driver has it in his

Below: Fireman John Guest (left) and driver David Rouse are no doubt realising a few ambitions as they work GWR 4-4-0 No 3440 *City of Truro* at Bishops Lydeard on 24 July 1992. Can David be thinking of Wellington Bank in 1904? *John Robinson*

possession. The staff will be given to the driver of the second or last train proceeding through the section and will be returned by a driver working in the opposite direction. Of course, the same situation could arise at the other end of the section but eventually all will return to normal and staffs will return to where they belong.

The 'Train Staff and Ticket' system is satisfactory so long as trains run in their normal paths and nothing unforeseen arises. However, the system is sadly deficient when all does not go according to plan. When that happens, something rather more sophisticated is required and such occasions are catered for with the 'Electric Key Token'. With this system, there is a large cabinet-like instrument at the end of each section, which contains a key usually made of aluminium, inscribed with the name of the section, eg Minehead-Blue Anchor, and designed in such a way that each section's keys will only fit the instruments at each end of the section to which they relate. There may be any number of these keys.

When a token, which is, like the staff, the driver's authority to proceed, is required, mutual co-operation between the signalmen at each end of the section allows one token only to be withdrawn to permit a train to proceed. The mechanism is so arranged that only one token may be out at any one time. No further tokens can be extracted until the original token has been returned to one or other of the instruments. As an additional safety measure, the signals are connected electrically with token instruments, so that a signal can only be lowered once when a token has been extracted.

The 'Electric Key Token' (EKT) working, if the rules are followed, is virtually foolproof. It allows complete flexibility of working, since trains can be sent up and down as required. Although this system is used at present only between Minehead and Blue Anchor, it is the company's intention to extend it eventually to Bishops Lydeard as resources permit.

When the line reopened in March 1976, trains ran only between Minehead and Blue Anchor. Since there are no facilities to pass trains at Dunster, 'One Train Working' was adopted and the service was, to all intents and purposes, a shuttle service. Blue Anchor has always been fully signalled and in those days trains ran into the up platform, all passengers disembarking. The engine uncoupled, ran round the train, shunted it up the line towards Washford and pulled it back into the down platform for passengers to entrain for the return trip. It was a simple 'there and back' operation. For this service, a single Minehead-Blue Anchor train staff was introduced.

Over the years, Minehead has seen quite a number of different arrangements for the operation of trains. From 1976 until 1991, entry to the station was controlled by a ground frame known as Minehead East Ground Frame. In addition to this, in 1976-77, a

Above: Driver Dick Wood awaits the right away on 1 January 1993 at Crowcombe Heathfield with the 13.45 service to Minehead. Motive power is provided by ex-GWR No 3205. *Stephen Edge*

two-lever frame was installed to allow run-round movements in the Main platform (platform 1). Since, at that time, there was no crossover from Main to Bay, any stock movements involved a trip to Dunster to use the crossover there.

In 1977, a new crossover was installed at Minehead allowing access to the Bay platform and it was at this time that the five-lever Minehead East Ground Frame was installed, giving access to Main or Bay. Two train staffs were available: Minehead Main–Blue Anchor RED would be released when the points were set and locked for the Main platform; Minehead Bay–Blue Anchor BLUE would be released when the points were set for the Bay platform. Obviously, only one could be released at any one time and strict discipline was necessary so that the system worked correctly. Owing to the lack of run-round facilities in the Bay, the normal practice was for locomotive-hauled trains to use the Main and diesel multiple-units the Bay.

The system mentioned above was in use until the commissioning of Minehead signalbox in 1990. 'Train Staff and Ticket' working was not permitted between

Minehead and Blue Anchor due to the inability to clear the section of the first train arrival. Therefore, when two trains were required to follow in the same direction the train staff would have to be brought by road from the station in advance – an almost daily occurrence.

For many years the Williton–Bishops Lydeard section was worked as 'One Engine in Steam'. However, with the alterations to the track layout at the latter station in 1993, the opportunity was taken to institute 'Train Staff and Ticket' working. A spring-loaded trap point installed in the up siding allowed a train arriving on a ticket to be locked in the up siding. This method of working continues between Crowcombe Heathfield and Bishops Lydeard but because there are at the time of writing no fixed signals at Bishops Lydeard, this working operates only when specially authorised.

With the commissioning of Crowcombe Heathfield signalbox, new arrangements were brought into being to operate the line between Williton and Bishops Lydeard, hitherto a single section of considerable distance. There are three train staffs: Bishops Lydeard–Williton BROWN, Bishops Lydeard-Crowcombe BLUE and Crowcombe–Williton RED. When Crowcombe box is 'switched out' (ie not in use), the two short section staffs are locked in Annetts key release instruments in Crowcombe box. The points are locked and running signals through the down loop are cleared for both directions.

To switch Crowcombe in, to shorten the section, the Bishops Lydeard–Williton staff must be taken to Crowcombe, either by road or by train, and the Bishops Lydeard–Williton staff inserted in its key release instrument. Signals may now be returned to danger. The signalman at Crowcombe can request 'line clear' from either Williton or, if a signalman is on duty, Bishops Lydeard and either Bishops Lydeard–Crowcombe or Crowcombe–Williton staff withdrawn. The Bishops Lydeard–Williton long staff is locked in its instrument until BOTH short section staffs are returned and locked in their key release instruments, when the box may be 'switched out' and long section working resumed.

With regard to Minehead's Seaward Way level crossing, for up trains, the crossing is fully automatic, operated by trains occupying and clearing track circuits. For down trains, since it is important that the points are set correctly on the station side of the crossing, the signalman must have set the route correctly and locked the points before clearing an aspect on the down home signal. Until the lever in the frame has been operated for this signal, the crossing will not operate. To proceed over the crossing in the down direction, the driver requires a 'proceed' aspect on the signal in addition to a white flashing light to inform him that the crossing is operating correctly.

Above: Fireman Barry Malcolm surrenders the BA-MD token to signalman Ron Williams at Minehead on 6 July 1991. Ex-GWR 2-6-2T No 6106 is at the head of the 15.45 service from Bishops Lydeard. *Stephen Edge*

When the present company took over the line in 1976, there were still minor road crossings with gates and cottages provided for their attendants. It was obviously quite impractical, if only on grounds of cost, to resurrect such methods of working, despite the desire to re-create a branch line atmosphere. Accordingly, it was decided that the gates would be abolished and the crossings would be open with flashing lights for both road and rail users, in accordance with current light railway practice. There are speed restrictions for trains at all these crossings and a duty of care is laid upon road users to exercise caution before crossing the railway line.

In total, there are five level crossings with lights, including the one at Minehead with half-barriers and one for pedestrians only at Watchet. Only one gatekeeper's cottage now remains: that at Sea Lane, Dunster and it is privately owned. The cottages at Leigh Woods and Roebuck Gate have been demolished by the present company to improve visibility for both road and rail. Road traffic is controlled by the usual double flashing red lights, while train drivers have a flashing white light to indicate that those controlling road traffic are functioning correctly and it is safe to proceed.

NOTE: The up direction indicates towards Taunton; the down direction, towards Minehead. Similar terminology applies to platforms.

Signalboxes

There are five signalboxes on the line: Minehead, Blue Anchor, Williton, Crowcombe Heathfield and Bishops Lydeard. The first four are fully operational, while that at Bishops Lydeard contains a full lever frame but has not yet been commissioned. Three of the boxes control road crossings.

The line is controlled from Minehead signalbox, the controller normally doubling as Minehead signalman. On special occasions, there may be two persons performing these functions. The box contains 26 levers (16 mechanical and 10 electrical), together with an electric key token instrument for the Minehead–Blue Anchor section. A demonstration token exchange apparatus has been installed outside the signalbox. It is the only one on the line, although there were several such installations in former days. Its primary function is to allow faster exchange of tokens than is possible with hand exchange (40mph as against 10mph) and the use of these devices enables timetables to be speeded up considerably on single lines.

Blue Anchor signalbox contains a 17-lever frame and a wheel to operate the crossing gates closing the road. Once a common sight, these mechanically operated gates are the last of their type in the West Country and one of the few sets still in use in the United Kingdom. The box also contains, as at Minehead, an electric key token instrument for the section to Minehead. The flexibility of working this gives is a boon at such busy events as 'Friends of Thomas the Tank Engine' weekends.

Williton box is the only remaining operational Bristol & Exeter Railway signalbox, although the 27-lever frame is of Great Western origin. The gates which close the road unusually operate outwards and are opened and closed by hand. This is because the crossing is what is known as an 'occupation crossing', the road being considered merely a service road after the opening of the new road which crosses the line by a bridge a little way south of the station.

Below: July 1994. Signalman Peter Vile watches as the Cravens-built DMU led by the Class 115 power car pulls into the newly-commissioned loop and platform at Crowcombe Heathfield. *Stephen Edge*

Some alterations have been made to the signalling at this station over the years. Shortly after reopening by the present company, the station was for a long time treated as a sort of frontier station, with passengers obliged to change trains here to proceed onwards to Minehead or Bishops Lydeard. Also in the early years a winter diesel service operated from here on certain days to and from Minehead to serve the local population. To avoid the need for a signalman when trains terminated here, the up platform was signalled for bi-directional working and all trains used this platform with the box being switched out. This arrangement has now been removed, but a backing signal may still be seen at the Minehead end of the up platform. This consists of a red arm with two holes in it and is used when it may be convenient to use platform 2 for arrival and departure of a train, for example, during Gala Days, when a special timetable may be in force.

Crowcombe Heathfield is the most recently commissioned of the railway's signalboxes. It is just over 15 miles from Minehead and about 5¾ miles from Williton. When the present company took over, all the signalling and indeed the box itself had been removed long ago. The entire installation has been rebuilt from scratch, entailing many thousands of hours' labour. The brick base of the box is new but the metal window-frames are GWR originals from Ebbw Vale Sidings South signalbox, as is the wooden superstructure. The 29-lever frame came from Frome

Above left: Signalman Ian Grady at the frame in Blue Anchor box. Note the wheel for operating the road crossing gates, lamp room (through window) and camping coaches. *Ian Wright*

Above: Ian Grady tackles the Minehead ground frame on 17 April 1993. *Stephen Edge*

North. The signalbox and loop were inspected and passed for passenger use by Major John Poyntz of HM Railway Inspectorate on 10 May 1994.

Although Bishops Lydeard signalbox survived the closure of the line in 1971, the lever frame had been removed prior to reopening. A certain amount of work has been carried out to the interior of the box, including the installation of a complete 33-lever frame. However, the station is not yet signalled and locomotive run-round facilities are controlled by two ground frames. For special events, a 'Person in Charge' (PIC) may be appointed to supervise train movements at this station. Major alterations are in hand for Bishops Lydeard which, when completed, will probably entail full signalling of the station and recommissioning of the signalbox.

AUTHOR'S NOTE: Grateful thanks are extended to Steve Martin, Operating Superintendent, West Somerset Railway, for his valuable assistance with the two preceding sections.

Above: Dunster station pictured in 1975; the anonymous signalbox is boarded up and the level crossing gates are firmly shut across the now derelict railway tracks. *Eric Rowlands*

Below: The gates, crossing keeper's cottage and lever frame hut at Leigh Woods level crossing all evince an air of almost terminal decline. *Eric Rowlands*

Above: On 30 May 1976, No 4561 is seen at Minehead, having been partially dismantled for restoration. Also visible are the two 0-6-0Ts, *Vulcan* and *Victor*, and the ex-GWR 0-6-0PT No 6412, a locomotive that was to bring revenue and fame to the railway through being used for a television series. *John Reeves*

Left: Bishops Lydeard pictured on 16 January 1993. Nos 4561 and 3205 double-head a special taking passengers from the HST, which had just brought an excursion off the main line. *Stephen Edge*

Right: The three ex-GWR tank engines, Nos 4561, 5542 and 5521, are pictured at Bishops Lydeard station on 7 March 1976. *John Reeves*

Locomotives

Steam Locos

The first locomotives to be acquired by the company were two 0-6-0 Bagnall saddle tanks named *Victor* and *Vulcan*. These were the surviving pair of an original trio (the third, *Valiant*, having been scrapped), built in 1950-51. They were enormous, extremely heavy locomotives, even by industrial standards and represented the zenith of industrial steam power. They were originally built for shunting in a South Wales steel works but prior to acquisition by the WSR had passed to the Austin Motor Co at Longbridge in the Midlands. Much work was done by Harry Lee and his gang in the bracing outdoor conditions of Taunton East Yard to return *Victor* to working condition in preparation for the reopening of the line, although it was not until 1977 that *Vulcan* returned to steam.

At this time, the company had the potential use of only one other unit of motive power. This was *Whitehead*, an 0-4-0 Peckett saddle tank. Neither the Peckett nor the two Bagnalls possessed vacuum brakes at that time, so they were quite unsuitable for hauling passenger trains. In the event, only the Bagnalls acquired vacuum brakes and the Peckett was fated to spend its short life on the line as Minehead shed pilot. Even then, it had limited use, soon giving way to the more convenient and economical diesel shunters.

As far back as 1974, Nos 4561 and 7820 *Dinmore Manor* had been reserved at Barry scrapyard by the railway for future use, the latter only in 1995 looking like being ready for further service after a lengthy and costly overhaul. Other ventures in the pipeline around this time were appeals for funds to purchase ex-GWR 2-6-2Ts Nos 5521 and 5542, and the Diesel & Electric Preservation Group's project with 'Hymek' No 7017. However, it was to be some years before any of these was to turn a wheel in active service. There was one other unit on offer: a small four-wheeled diesel-mechanical shunter from Unigate Dairies at Chard. This was built by Ruston Hornsby as works number 183062 in 1937.

It is astonishing, looking back with the accumulated wisdom of a quarter of a century, that running a branch line with its attendant gradients using the two Bagnalls was ever seriously contemplated. While they were adequate for a four-trains-a-day service to Blue Anchor and back and with decent watering facilities could just about cope with the Williton run, they very soon demonstrated their (and the infrastructure's) shortcomings once running beyond Williton became a reality. They were also, amongst other things, extremely heavy on the permanent way.

In the meantime, with the company's finances not stretching to the purchase of anything of consequence, the association purchased ex-GWR

0-6-0PT No 6412 from the Dart Valley Railway. This, providentially, was in full working order, which was just as well, bearing in mind the reduced circumstances in which the line was shortly to find itself. This small locomotive has become a mascot of the WSR, having been on the line longer than any other steam locomotive. It is undergoing a complete overhaul at the time of writing.

During the years prior to reopening, the Somerset & Dorset Railway Museum Trust had been collecting locomotives, including ex-Somerset & Dorset Joint Railway No 88 (LMS 13808, BR 53808), although here again, none was in a steamable condition and none was to be so for a very long time.

For the first 10 years, the only regular passenger steam power on the West Somerset Railway were the two Bagnalls and No 6412 and very rarely indeed, if at all, were all three in service or even available for service, at the same time. The gods certainly smiled on the WSR in those years and the subsequent transformation has been almost unbelievable, with the entire service being maintained by mainline steam locomotives.

Above left: On 15 April 1976 ex-GWR Pannier tank No 6412 is captured taking water at Minehead. *John Reeves*

Centre left: No 53808's official 'return to steam' working took place during the Gala Week in September 1987. On 13 September the locomotive departs from Stogumber with the 09.45 Minehead-Bishops Lydeard service — the official working that marked its restoration to service. *Stephen Edge*

Below: Hauling a short demonstration freight, ex-GWR 0-6-0 No 3205 is pictured near Blue Anchor with the 15.44 Williton-Minehead service on 4 September 1991. *Peter Chatman*

Above: The last steam locomotive built for British Railways, Class 9F No 92220, spent a period on loan to the West Somerset Railway. It is caught in August 1989 entering Crowcombe station. *Stephen Edge*

A steam locomotive which did a very limited amount of passenger work on the line during the mid-1980s was Hudswell Clarke 0-6-0T *Jennifer*. For various reasons, this engine only worked during one season and was then retired from service. This was partly due to the increased weight of the trains, when *Jennifer* suffered from much the same shortcomings as her stablemates of the time, *Victor* and *Vulcan*,
ie limited coal and water capacity, together with steam production problems. *Jennifer* lay out of use on the line for some years, not finally leaving until 1993.

1986 was the first year the line had a visiting engine. This was an ex-GWR 2-6-2T No 5572, a 'Small Prairie' and sister engine to No 4561. The difference between this locomotive and those used hitherto was most marked and from that year a large number of steam locomotives from other sources have visited the line, usually for the summer season. No 5572 was urgently required once again the following year to bail out a struggling locomotive department, which was having trouble with *Victor*.

The 1987 summer service was run with Nos 5572, 6412 and *Victor* and it speaks volumes for all those involved that they managed to keep the service going with such minimal motive power. However, one should state at this point that the DEPG had occasionally come to the rescue of an ailing motive power stud with the loan of one of their own units, particularly one of the Class 14 diesels.

During the third week in August 1987, ex-SDJR 2-8-0 No 88 finally returned to service. This was the culmination of years of effort: fund-raising, heavy engineering, scraping, painting and 1001 other jobs which all go into steam locomotive restoration. In the ensuing years this fine locomotive has more than proved its worth and has served the West Somerset Railway in exemplary fashion. Although it runs on an ex-GWR line, it is rightly regarded as something of a 'flagship' engine and will pull almost anything hung behind it.

Another steam locomotive returned to service in time to run 'Santa Specials'; ex-GWR No 3205, formerly on the Severn Valley Railway, had been completely overhauled and has since proved a mainstay of the fleet. Meanwhile, *Victor* had been laid up and a buyer was being actively sought.

On 23 May 1988, *Victor* departed the WSR for a new life on the Strathspey Railway in Scotland. It was a nostalgic moment, especially for those whose memories went back to the early days of the revived WSR and even before that. However, there was little doubt that there was now no place for such locomotives on the railway, as the train service had developed quite beyond their capacity. *Victor* had pulled the very first train out of Minehead on 28 March 1976.

The summer 1988 service was run between Nos 88, 3205 and 6412. Although the heavier trains were too much to entrust to No 6412, it was often to be seen hauling the prestigious 'Quantock Belle' dining train, which was an ideal load for this small locomotive.

The West Somerset Railway welcomed the largest locomotive ever seen on the line to date on 11 March 1989, when BR 2-10-0 No 92220 *Evening Star* arrived for the season from the National Railway Museum. No 92220, built in 1960 at Swindon Works, was the last steam locomotive constructed for British Railways. It spent the rest of the season on the line and was undoubtedly responsible for a record year on the railway in all respects. Up to the beginning of October, the line carried an increase of

passengers of 31.7% over the previous year.

Somewhat overshadowed by the advent of *Evening Star* was an event which cannot be allowed to pass unremarked. This was the return to service in September of ex-GWR 2-6-2T No 4561. This engine had been on the line since the very early days and like No 88, thanks to a lot of very hard work and dedication by a small team led by Bill Monteith, it was now rightly taking its place in the WSR steam stud. It has performed well since and is well able to power the majority of service trains.

1990 was a quiet year so far as new developments were concerned, and the next noteworthy event took place the following year, when another ex-GWR 2-6-2T No 6106 (a so-called 'Large Prairie' because of its six large driving wheels) arrived from the Great Western Society's depot at Didcot to assist with that

year's summer timetable. The service that summer was run with Nos 6106, 3205, 4561, 6412 and 88, although, of course, not all were available for service simultaneously. No 6106 returned to the line once again, in 1993, to assist with the summer service.

The next year, 1992, saw ex-GWR 2-8-0 No 3822 visiting the line for the summer season. It appeared in its wartime black livery, complete with blanked-out cab windows. This year celebrated 150 years of railways at Taunton and was marked also by short visits of *Locomotion* and the record-making locomotive *City of Truro*, which stayed on the railway from 29 June to mid-August, when it returned to the National Railway Museum. A popular performer, it was responsible for bringing extra visitors to the line.

Once again, for the 1993 summer season, No 6106

Left: Ex-GWR 2-6-2T No 6106 and 'Hymek' No D7018 pass Williton down distant signal on Castle Hill with the 15.45 Minehead-Bishops Lydeard train. *Stephen Edge*

Below left: On 3 May 1992 ex-GWR 2-8-0 No 3822 coasts downhill at Sampford Brett Bridge with the 12.20 Bishops Lydeard-Minehead train. Note the fireman damping down the coal. *Stephen Edge*

Right: Driver Don Haynes seems to be waiting for a lift at Norton Fitzwarren. The Great Western main line is in the background. *South West Counties Newspapers*

was hired from Didcot to ease a locomotive shortage. Also visiting the railway for the season was ex-LMSR '8F' 2-8-0 No 48773. On 6 August, ex-GWR 2-6-2T No 4160 re-entered traffic.

There were two guest locomotives for 1994. The first was BR Class 4 4-6-0 No 75069. The arrival of this engine was a historical milestone, since it hauled a special train originating at Peterborough direct from Worcester to Minehead. This was the first time since the line was closed in 1971 that such an excursion had taken place.

The second visiting locomotive during 1994 was ex-GWR 4-6-0 No 7802 *Bradley Manor*. This engine was involved in the railway's first fatal accident on 12 September, when travelling tender-first on an ex-Bishops Lydeard train at Ker Moor, between Blue Anchor and Dunster. The deceased was not a passenger nor member of staff but a lady trespasser on the line attempting to save her wandering dog. This is a graphic illustration that *all* railways are potentially lethal places and should be treated with respect. An ancient steam locomotive travelling at 25mph can be just as dangerous as an HST doing 125mph.

During 1995, steam services were run using Nos 88, 4561, 4160 and visiting locomotive ex-GWR 4-6-0 No 7828 *Odney Manor*. Being overhauled, but expected back in traffic before the end of the year, were Nos 6412, 3205 and ex-GWR 4-6-0 No 7820 – *Dinmore Manor*. A surprise visitor to the line in June was ex-BR No 71000 *Duke of Gloucester*, which was offered a temporary home after some difficulties on the Paignton & Dartmouth Railway precluded the engine remaining there. Despite the enormous weight of this locomotive (154 tons with tender), permission was sought and obtained from the authorities to run a few special trains with it. It certainly proved a most popular crowd-puller. As a result of a particularly hot summer during the year, many steam specials on the main line were cancelled

and this meant No 71000 remained on the WSR for the remainder of the season. Since resident steam power was again somewhat sparse, the *Duke of Gloucester*'s visit turned out to be a most fortunate happening. The 'Duke' finally left the line in late September, having worked over 1,000 miles in service. It was a happy experience for all concerned.

Dinmore Manor returned to traffic during the summer, just in time to relieve a distressed *Odney Manor*, which had retired with firebox trouble. The timing was most fortuitous, enabling *Dinmore Manor* to provide a 'Manor' presence at the autumn Steam Gala, 15/17 September, although the hoped-for 'Manor' double-heading did not, unfortunately, materialise.

It was recorded in *On-Line*, the house newsletter, that the '7F' No 88 had now clocked up over 40,000 miles in service on the WSR.

At the end of the 1995 season, it was reported that Nos 4160, 7820 and 88 were available for service, work was proceeding on Nos 4561, 7828, 3205 and 5542, while the association was still labouring to reassemble No 6412 in Williton shed.

Diesel Units

Since the earliest days, the West Somerset Railway has used a combination of steam and diesel motive power. There were two main reasons for this: the first was that originally the company envisaged running a commuter service to and from Taunton using diesel multiple-units and the second was the more pragmatic one of shortage of motive power! There is now, of course, a third reason: that diesel motive power itself is becoming historic in its own right.

The very first diesel units to be used by the new company had been acquired long before the reopening of the line. These were two two-car Park Royal sets, ex-BR Nos W50413/4 and W56168/9. These did sterling service for many years, sometimes

Left: Ex-GWR 'Manor' class 4-6-0 No 7828 *Odney Manor* hauls the 10.25 Bishops Lydeard-Minehead service at Blue Anchor on 28 May 1995. The station has been brought up to its present standard mainly by volunteer labour. *Stephen Edge*

Centre left: On 18 September 1994 ex-GWR 'Manor' class 4-6-0 No 7802 *Bradley Manor* was employed on the line. It is seen leaving Williton with a working from Minehead to Bishops Lydeard. *Stephen Edge*

Below: Formed of a two-car DMU, the 12.30 Minehead-Watchet service was extended to Williton on 17 February 1978 due to the bad weather and the lack of bus services. The train is pictured entering Washford station. *Stephen Edge*

Above right: An Easter Monday relief service is pictured at Stones Wood on 17 April 1995. The train is formed of DMUs from both Classes 105 and 117. Note the recent clearance of undergrowth which has led to improved views. *Stephen Edge*

Right: Class 14 No 9551 is pictured at Bishops Lydeard with Dave Williams at the controls. *Bob Tiller*

running in multiple, particularly on Saturday morning services from Minehead, when holidaymakers returning to Taunton had to be carried in large numbers. Two of these coaches have now been scrapped but one complete set survives, destined when restored to be the only surviving Park Royal unit in working order. The usual problem of asbestos insulation and its removal arose, so it was decided to retain the two more serviceable cars, which resulted in the pairing now of Nos W50414 and W56168. Although originally owned by the company, this DMU has now been sold to the Diesel & Electric Preservation Group, based at Williton.

Another early arrival on the line was 'Hymek' No D7017. This was not in working order initially but was overhauled and put back into service, minus its train heating boiler, in 1977 and has been used many times since. It is a valuable member of the loco stud and is more than capable of standing in for steam locomotives. It is a regular performer at Diesel Gala Weekends, along with sister No D7018.

Class 14 0-6-0 No D9526 was the next mainline diesel unit to arrive, on 3 April 1980. This, too, has been a useful performer, standing in for DMU stock and even the occasional steam train.

In recent years, three other diesel multiple-units have worked on the line: a Gloucester set, a Cravens set and a Class 115 set. The first named is temporarily in store and the DMU service is worked principally by the Cravens set. It is hoped that all the above, in addition to the Park Royals, will be preserved for use in due course.

Several small shunting locomotives have been in evidence since the early years. The first ex-BR type to arrive was No D2994. This has seen extensive use as yard pilot at Minehead and on the occasional works train. It is now on loan to the Avon Valley Railway. Ex-BR Class 04s Nos D2271 and D2205 are also extensively used. Only in 1994 did the railway acquire its own Class 08 No 08850 (ex-No D4018).

Williton depot is now home to a large variety of diesel locomotive power, including Class 52 No D1035 *Western Yeoman* (formerly No D1010 *Western Campaigner*), Class 35 'Hymek' No D7018, Class 14 No D9551 and the latest arrival, Class 50 No 50149 *Defiance*, in addition to those locomotives described in the above paragraphs. The result is that, together with the current impressive line-up of steam power, the railway is well able to cope with intensive services over the entire line, as well as react positively to any contingencies which may arise; a far cry from the situation which obtained for the first 10 years of the company's existence.

The West Somerset Railway now successfully runs trains on over 200 days of the year and these trains cover a distance of over 250,000 vehicle miles each year.

Following another highly successful 1995 autumn Diesel Gala, with a number of visiting locomotives, it was announced that 'Peak' No D120 was to remain on the line for a further 12 months.

Left: One of the regular jobs on any railway is the operation of a weedkilling train. Here, on 22 June 1981, the Class 07 diesel No D2994 is seen with the WSR's weedkilling train at Bishops Lydeard. *Stephen Edge*

Below: Power to spare. Class 50 No 50149 is pictured at Williton whilst heading to Minehead to recover a 'dead' DMU on 17 June 1995. *Peter Thompson*

Bottom: Pictured arriving at Bishops Lydeard during the Easter of 1980, 'Hymek' No 7017 hauls an impressive rake of coaching stock. Next to the locomotive is an ex-GWR Siphon G van. *Stephen Edge*

Carriage and Wagon

Lines such as the West Somerset invariably attract a wide variety of carriages and wagons, in much the same way as locomotives. This line is no exception to the rule and over the years many and varied items of rolling stock have arrived and departed. Today the company operates a policy whereby, generally speaking, all rolling stock must earn its keep. The main reason for this is that, as will be observed by a trip along the line, siding and storage space is at a premium and there is simply no room for rows of carriages and wagons awaiting restoration, which may be calculated in years, rather than months. There are, of course, rare exceptions to this rule, such as the historic GWR first-class sleeping car in the care of the Steam Trust.

For reopening, seven passenger coaches of various types were acquired; two were purchased by the West Somerset Railway Association Stock Fund, the company being at that time somewhat financially embarrassed. These vehicles may be described as follows:

Tourist Second Open (TSO) No 4039, built at Swindon in 1955 and ex-Southern Region of BR; TSO No 4493, built at York in 1956 and ex-Eastern Region; TSO No 4602, built at York in 1956; TSO No 4346, built at Birmingham in 1956; Second Open (SO) No 4814, built at Birmingham in 1959; Brake Second Open (BSO) No 9278, built at Doncaster in 1956, ex-Eastern Region; Second Compartment (SK) No 24307, built at Eastleigh in 1951, ex-Southern Region. The WSRA Stock Fund owned Nos 4493 and 4602.

Many ex-BR Mark 1 coaches have since been acquired and some other stock with specialist application is in service. There are two buffet cars and one vehicle of which the railway is most proud:

Below: Peckett 0-4-0ST *Kilmersdon* hauls a short goods train past Blue Anchor up distant signal bound for Minehead on 18 September 1993. *Stephen Edge*

see occasional use, they were soon sold out of service.

Among the more interesting and historical items of coaching stock on the line are three former camping coaches, all ex-GWR, which were brought on to the line in 1976. Their former numbers had been 3639, 3668 and 2578. They were built in 1910 (the first two) and 1914. The GWR renumbered them as camping coaches 9887, 9888 and 9889 respectively. All are thought to have been used in France during World War 1, probably as ambulance coaches. They ended their days at Blue Anchor under BR auspices.

In 1979 five privately-purchased first-class Pullman cars arrived on the line. These splendid vehicles comprised two parlour cars and three kitchen cars. They ran for some years as 'The Quantock Pullman' (their modern equivalent is 'The Quantock Belle') but were eventually moved to the North York Moors Railway and later the Severn Valley Railway. The first time they ran in service, *Victor* was the motive power and attempting to serve soup or wine as the locomotive 'boxed' its way along the line from Minehead to Bishops Lydeard was not an experience to be repeated voluntarily by either staff or passengers!

A large number of freight vehicles have been seen at one time or another on the WSR. Another book would be required to do justice to the subject. However, mention must be made of the very first item of freight stock to be used by the present company, although it is actually owned by the association. This is a four-wheel covered van built in 1939 by the GWR to diagram Y9 under lot 1606. It was purchased in 1975 for use on the line, after being condemned at Taunton in 1972. It is still used on the line and its running number is 150346.

Full details of all locomotives and rolling stock on the line are to be found in the *Stock Book*, which may be purchased from retail outlets along the line.

the 'Lorna Doone' coach for the disabled and those accompanying them. This is believed to be the only coach of its type anywhere in the United Kingdom and it incorporates hydraulic lifts for easy wheelchair access, together with special lavatory facilities. There has also been a first/second-class composite and one Mark 2 coach. However, both these have been taken out of service for various reasons and await disposal.

All coaching stock is of the corridor type, but in earlier years there were some non-gangwayed second-class compartment coaches. They arrived in 1979 but were not popular, particularly with guards and travelling ticket inspectors (TTIs). While they did

Opposite left: The interior of the 1897 GWR sleeping car illustrates two things: the remarkable state of preservation and how much remains to be done. The date is 1 August 1992. *David Mark*

Below left: A newly-acquired steel dropside wagon pictured at Bishops Lydeard siding on 16 November 1993. *Peter Thompson*

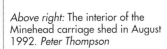

Above right: The interior of the Minehead carriage shed in August 1992. *Peter Thompson*

Centre right: Carriage & Wagon foreman Andy Hurley pictured at work on the new (converted from a Mark 1 FO) buffet coach in platform 1 at Minehead on 14 March 1990. *Peter Thompson*

Below right: Lack of covered accommodation does not deter volunteers. Restoration work going on with the Park Royal DMU is illustrated; Roy Jones is up the ladder on 6 March 1993. *Peter Thompson*

The first timetable produced for reopening in March 1976 was a simple buff-coloured slip measuring 17.5cm by 10cm. There were also large posters placed in prominent positions around the area. The first timetable in what might be called the modern format appeared for the 1977 season. From the very first timetables, samples of fares were given.

In former years, a winter service was run for local users. This service ran between Minehead and Williton, utilising a DMU set. A separate timetable was issued for the winter service, which, in those times, ran every day between the end of the summer season one year and the beginning of the summer season the next. The winter timetable is reproduced.

No through service was run until 9 June 1979 and even then it was confined to a Saturday diesel service of three through trains a day. Although there was a steam service to Bishops Lydeard from Minehead with effect from 10 June of that year, the 'frontier mentality' prevailed and passengers were obliged to change at Williton for both outward and return journeys, a state of affairs that was to continue for some years, primarily due to the inadequacies of the locomotive fleet.

It was to be many years before regular scheduled steam haulage appeared on Saturday trains on the WSR: 15 years after reopening, to be exact, and they made their first appearance in the 1991 timetable. In the meantime, timetables of amazing complexity had begun to appear, culminating in not only a passenger's nightmare but one for those who had to implement it as well! The 1986 timetable is typical and is reproduced.

By the mid-1980s the timetables had begun to assume the format so well known today. The 1986 edition was a grand affair, announcing the railway's 10th anniversary on its cover. Produced in colour, it took the shape of an A3 sheet of paper when fully unfolded and the inside contained photographs and a description of the line. The railway had by now adopted the slogan 'Better by Miles'. These full-colour timetables are expensive to produce and financial considerations in recent years have meant that their issue has been mainly confined to Tourist Information Offices, principal main line railway outlets and other commercial organisations. Until 1995, passengers were issued individually with monochrome timetables. However, in that year, the decision was taken to publish and issue only ones in colour.

In an effort to simplify matters for passengers, many of whom never travel by train and equally many of whom never use public transport in any form, the timetable has been reduced to what is considered its simplest form, using extensive colour-coding.

As the railway has recovered from the vicissitudes of its lean years, various additional attractions have been mounted, each requiring its own timetable. A perennial favourite is the 'Santa Special'. All the 'preserved' lines now operate these trains but the WSR is so long that two separate services are offered, tapping custom at both ends of the line. Santa's Grottos are set up at Crowcombe Heathfield and Blue Anchor and return trains are run on several days before Christmas (Saturdays and Sundays). Adults are welcomed and seasonal refreshments are offered to all travellers. Seats are bookable in advance on these popular trains and they are normally steam-hauled.

Gala Weekends are now a regular feature of the WSR, with both steam and diesel haulage, although not usually mixed. Intensive timetables are operated and additional attractions offered, such as pick-up goods trains. Another popular feature of these weekends is the Norton Shuttle, on which a train takes those so wishing down to the WSR boundary with BR at Norton Fitzwarren, where passing main

Left: The winter 1976 timetable.

WEST SOMERSET RAILWAY

WINTER TIMETABLE: 25th SEPTEMBER UNTIL FURTHER NOTICE

		Mondays to Saturdays					Sundays until 31 Oct		NOTES
		TFSO	X	@ St			St	St	
MINEHEAD	dep	7.20	9.15	12.30	3.00	4.20	5.55	12.30	3.00	
DUNSTER	dep	7.25	9.20	12.35	3.07	4.25	6.00	12.37	3.07	TFSO = Tuesdays, Fridays and Saturdays only
BLUE ANCHOR	dep	7.34	9.30	12.45	3.20	4.35	6.10	12.50	3.20	
WASHFORD	dep	7.40	9.37	12.52	3.30	4.42	6.17	1.00	3.30	
WATCHET	dep	7.48	9.45	1.00	3.37	4.50	6.25	1.07	3.37	
WILLITON	arr	7.53	9.50	1.05	3.45	4.55	6.30	1.15	3.45	St = Scheduled for Steam haulage
		TFSO	X	@ St			St	St	
WILLITON	dep	7.58	9.55	1.55	4.05	5.00	6.35	1.35	4.05	X = 24 Sept - 30 Oct. May be steam hauled; if so journey time 10 minutes longer each way
WATCHET	dep	8.04	10.00	2.00	4.15	5.05	6.40	1.45	4.15	
WASHFORD	dep	8.11	10.08	2.08	4.25	5.13	6.48	1.55	4.25	
BLUE ANCHOR	dep	8.20	10.18	2.18	4.35	5.23	6.58	2.05	4.35	
DUNSTER	dep	8.26	10.24	2.24	4.42	5.29	7.04	2.12	4.42	@ = Daily 24 Sept - 30 Oct only
MINEHEAD	arr	8.33	10.30	2.30	4.50	5.35	7.10	2.20	4.50	

If train times are not convenient please tell us.
This Railway wants to serve you.

FARES TO AND FROM MINEHEAD

	Cheap Day Return	Stored Journey Tickets: 10 Journeys, either direction	
Williton	85p		£3.75
Watchet	80p		£3.50
Washford	65p		£2.75
Blue Anchor	50p		£2.25

Valid by all trains. Details of other cheap tickets on request

The Company reserves the right to amend or cancel this Timetable without notice. It is hoped the line can stay open throughout the Winter if trains are well used.

****IT'S YOUR RAILWAY - USE IT AND KEEP IT!****
Minehead Station (Tel: 4996)

September 1976 TTB2/76

Mondays to Fridays 8 June—22 July

TABLE 3		Ⓢ	TWFO Watchet Explorer	Ⓢ	Ⓢ			MThO
MINEHEAD	dep.	09.15	**10.35**	11.25	12.30	**14.35**	**15.40**	16.30	17.45
Dunster	dep.	09.20	**10.41**	11.30	12.35	**14.41**	**15.46**	16.35	17.50
Blue Anchor	arr.	09.26	**10.48**	11.36	12.41	**14.48**	**15.53**	16.41	17.56
	dep.	09.27		11.37	12.42			16.42	17.57
Washford	dep.	09.34		11.44	12.49			16.49	18.04
Watchet	dep.	09.41		11a51	12.56			16.56	18a10
Williton	arr.	09.46		—	13.01			17.01	—
				TWFO					MThO
Williton	dep.	09.55		—	13.55			17.05	
Watchet	dep.	10.01		11.55	14.01			17.11	18.15
Washford	dep.	10.08		12.02	14.08			17.18	18.22
Blue Anchor	arr.	10.14		12.08	14.14			17.24	18.28
	dep.	10.15	**11.05**	12.10	14.15	**15.05**	**16.10**	17.25	18.29
Dunster	dep.	10.21	**11.13**	12.16	14.21	**15.13**	**16.18**	17.31	18.35
MINEHEAD	arr.	10.27	**11.19**	12.22	14.27	**15.19**	**16.24**	17.37	18.40

TWFO—Tuesdays, Wednesdays, Fridays only   MThO—Mondays, Thursdays only

Mondays to Fridays 25 July—9 September

TABLE 4			TWFO Watchet Explorer	MThO			Ⓢ	Ⓢ		MThO
MINEHEAD	dep.	09.15	**10.35**	11.25	11.40	12.30	**14.35**	**15.40**	16.30	17.45
Dunster	dep.	09.20	**10.41**	11.30	11.46	12.35	**14.41**	**15.46**	16.35	17.50
Blue Anchor	arr.	09.26	**10.48**	11.36	11.53	12.41	**14.48**	**15.53**	16.41	17.56
	dep.	09.27		11.37		12.42			16.42	17.57
Washford	dep.	09.34		11.44		12.49			16.49	18.04
Watchet	dep.	09.41		11a51		12.56			16.56	18a10
Williton	arr.	09.46		—		13.01			17.01	—
				TWFO	MThO					MThO
Williton	dep.	09.55		—	13.55				17.05	— f
Watchet	dep.	10.01		11.55	14.01				17.11	18.15
Washford	dep.	10.08		12.02	14.08				17.18	18.22
Blue Anchor	arr.	10.14		12.08	14.14				17.24	18.28
	dep.	10.15	**11.05**	12.10	14.15	**15.05**	**16.10**		17.25	18.29
Dunster	dep.	10.21	**11.13**	12.16	14.21	**15.13**	**16.18**		17.31	18.35
MINEHEAD	arr.	10.27	**11.19**	12.22	14.27	**15.19**	**16.24**		17.37	18.40

Mondays to Fridays 12 September—7 October

TABLE 5			Ⓢ	Ⓢ		
MINEHEAD	dep.	09.15	12.30	**14.35**	**15.40**	16.30
Dunster	dep.	09.20	12.35	**14.41**	**15.46**	16.35
Blue Anchor	arr.	09.26	12.41	**14.48**	**15.53**	16.41
	dep.	09.27	12.42			16.42
Washford	dep.	09.34	12.49			16.49
Watchet	dep.	09.41	12.56			16.51
Williton	arr.	09.46	13.01			17.06
Williton	dep.	09.55	13.55			17.05
Watchet	dep.	10.01	14.01			17.11
Washford	dep.	10.08	14.08			17.18
Blue Anchor	arr.	10.14	14.14			17.24
	dep.	10.15	14.15	**15.05**	**16.10**	17.25
Dunster	dep.	10.21	14.21	**15.13**	**16.18**	17.31
MINEHEAD	arr.	10.27	14.27	**15.19**	**16.24**	17.37

Table 4 (above)
TWFO Tuesdays
                Wednesdays
                Fridays only
MThO Mondays
                Thursdays only

Ⓢ This symbol means
that the train is
STEAM HAULED
Wherever possible the
locomotive used will
be the TV star, "The
FLOCKTON FLYER".

Above: The 1977 timetable.

Below: The 1986 timetable cover.

Right: A typical gala event timetable.

TAKE THE
West Somerset Railway
TO MINEHEAD

BRITAIN'S LONGEST PRESERVED RAILWAY!
BISHOP'S LYDEARD to MINEHEAD
Superb Scenery........Sea & Sand
Nine Preserved Stations
Steam Locos. Museums Displays
BETTER BY MILES!

line trains may be observed. Passengers have to remain on board for this service, for there is, as yet, no station at Norton. A typical timetable is illustrated.

The latest innovation, which came rather late to the WSR, are the 'Friends of Thomas the Tank Engine' Weekends. No fewer than eight shuttle trips to Blue Anchor are run on this weekend, this being an ideal length of return trip for small children, whose boredom threshold is sometimes easily reached. These weekends have proved so popular, that the railway now holds one in the spring/summer and one in the autumn.

Now that diesel locomotives are becoming so much rarer on the main line, Diesel Gala Weekends attract large crowds and not just enthusiasts. During the October 1994 event, seven through return trains were run, together with a return goods working and one Blue Anchor shuttle, plus three Bishops Lydeard–Norton Fitzwarren shuttles. Timetables such as this call for some smart work in the operating department and all concerned have to be on their toes. In this connection, the new loop at Crowcombe Heathfield has made possible things undreamt of only a short time ago.

For readers interested in old timetables, certain ones may be available from: The Archivist, West Somerset Steam Railway Trust, The Railway Station, Williton, Somerset TA4 4RQ.

SPRING GALA WEEKEND.
SATURDAY 30th APRIL 1994

		Steam	Steam	Diesel	Steam	Steam	Diesel	DMU	Steam
Minehead	d	09.40	10.30	12.35	13.35	14.25	15.35	17.00	18.00
Dunster	d	09.46	10.34	12.41	13.41	14.31	15.41	17.06	18.06
Blue Anchor		09.54	10.44	12.47	13.49	14.40	15.46	17.12	18.14
	d	09.55	10.45	stop	13.50		15.47	17.13	18.15
Washford		10.04	10.54	13.01	13.59	—	15.53	17.21	18.23
Watchet		10.12	11.02	13.07	14.07	—	15.59	17.29	18.31
Doniford Beach (R)		10.15	11.06	13.10	14.10	—	16.02	17.31	18.34
Williton		10.19	11.09	13.12	14.15	—	16.04	17.33	18.38
	d	10.24	stop	13.13	14.24	—	16.09	stop	18.44
Stogumber	d	10.37	—	13.23	14.37	—	16.19	—	18.57
Crowcombe Heathfield	d	10.48	—	13.29	14.48	—	16.26	—	19.08
Bishops Lydeard		10.58	—	13.39	14.58	—	16.35	—	19.18
	d	—	—	—	—	—	—	—	—
Norton Fitzwarren	a	—	—	—	—	—	—	—	—

		Diesel	Steam	Steam	Diesel	Steam	Steam	DMU	Steam
Norton Fitzwarren	d	—	—	—	—	—	—	—	—
Bishops Lydeard	a	—	—	—	—	—	—	—	—
	d	09.55	—	11.20	13.50	—	15.30	—	18.10
Crowcombe Heathfield		10.05	—	11.35	14.00	—	15.45	—	18.25
Stogumber		10.12	—	11.44	14.07	—	15.54	—	18.34
Williton		10.21	—	11.53	14.15	—	16.03	—	18.43
	d	10.26	11.25	11.54	14.23	—	16.10	17.50	18.44
Doniford Beach (R)		10.28	11.29	11.58	14.25	—	16.14	17.52	18.48
Watchet		10.31	11.33	12.02	14.29	—	16.18	17.56	19.01
Washford		10.39	11.41	12.10	14.37	—	16.26	18.03	19.09
Blue Anchor	a	10.45	11.48	12.18	14.43	—	16.34	18.11	19.17
	d	10.50	11.49	12.21	14.46	15.15	16.35	18.17	19.18
Dunster		10.56	11.56	12.27	14.52	15.21	16.41	18.23	19.24
Minehead	a	11.02	12.02	12.34	14.58	15.29	16.48	18.29	19.30

BUS LINK SERVICE

Taunton Castleway	d	09.15	10.40	13.10	14.40	17.50
Taunton BR Station	d	09.25	10.50	13.20	14.50	17.15
Bishops Lydeard	a	09.45	11.10	13.40	15.10	17.35
Bishops Lydeard	d	—	11.15	13.45	15.15	17.40
Taunton BR Station	a	—	11.35	14.05	15.35	17.55
Taunton Castleway	a	—	11.45	14.15	15.45	18.00

77

For the reopening of the line in 1976, locally printed card tickets were provided for journeys between Minehead and Blue Anchor, although no printed stock was available either for journeys to or from Dunster or for single fares; it was assumed, rightly or wrongly, that those who departed would return! These tickets were slightly larger than normal Edmondson size and this caused booking office staff some difficulty when removing them from ticket racks. However, dating on the traditional ticket dating press was possible. The last survivors of these local prints were the white Dog/Cycle tickets which continued in use long after the decision had been taken to carry accompanied bicycles free of charge.

These first tickets were buff in colour and contained only the fare values. No destination was shown.

Since 1977, practically all card tickets have been printed to the correct Edmondson specification, initially by the erstwhile BR ticket printing division at Crewe and latterly on ex-BR presses in the WSR's own printing shop at Dunster station. In addition to WSR tickets, the company also accepts contracts to print tickets for other organisations and in fact printed the tickets for the inaugural passenger train through the Channel Tunnel.

In 1977, a scheme was devised whereby single and return tickets were printed for journeys of predetermined fare values without mention of any station of origin or destination. The intention was to save on printing costs by identifying the issuing station by means of a code included in the date stamp, ie MD for Minehead, BA for Blue Anchor, etc. Although ingenious, the system did not make the task of ticket inspectors easy and it was abandoned soon afterwards when normal pre-printed stock was reintroduced. Current ticket styles follow an early BR design and colour scheme of buff card for returns and the much later BR style of white card printed in red for single fares. Family returns for selected journeys are on pink card in the 'Out and back' format. Ticket stocks are held in the booking offices at Minehead, Dunster, Blue Anchor, Watchet, Williton and Bishops Lydeard, while passengers boarding at other stations are provided with tickets issued from a Setright machine by guards or ticket inspectors on the train.

A novel feature for a private line was the Ten Journey Ticket available for several years in the mid-1970s and which allowed local residents and visitors to make 10 journeys in either direction between given stations at a 30% discount. These tickets were particularly popular with the regular passengers travelling to work in Watchet during the time of the commuter service in 1976. Local residents and members of the association continue to be able to travel at discounted fares by purchasing a 'Starcard'; on introduction, this scheme was known as membership of the Rail Users' Association.

After the line was reopened to Stogumber, day excursion facilities were offered, combining a mixture of steam and diesel mileage and three breaks of journey. In view of the differential fares charged at that time for steam and diesel travel, special lilac-coloured tickets were printed for these journeys. Although all tickets for DMU-operated services were at the time Setright machine issues, the opening to Bishops Lydeard was marked by the printing of 'Out and back' tickets to Taunton carrying the words 'Reduced Rate' and covering the rail journey to Bishops Lydeard and the special coach or bus connection to Taunton town centre.

During the first three years of operations, the company produced an astonishing array of platform tickets, including designs based on LNER, Great Northern Railway (Ireland) and British Railways originals. Many of these were sold only to collectors as a means of boosting revenue and indeed more than one series was produced for stations such as Washford and Stogumber, which have never enjoyed booking office facilities in WSR days. The most recent design is a hybrid based on a GNR(I) style with the familiar 'red diamond' overprint.

A few special tickets have been issued over the years. The first train on 28 March 1976 had a special souvenir ticket issued. In 1992, another special ticket was instituted to cater for round trips from certain stations to Stogumber to include entry fee for Bee World near that station.

Apart from staff proceeding to and from their place of work who travel free using their Staff Identity Card, there are two other methods of legitimate ticket-less travel. These take the form of Gold and Silver Passes. The former allows free and unlimited travel for life on scheduled trains for the holder and three others. To be eligible one must hold 20,000 shares in the company. Conditions for the latter are similar, except that only one other may accompany the holder and eligibility is 10,000 shares.

Special blue tickets are issued to association members upon production of a current membership card. Members are permitted two free days' unlimited travel on the railway on scheduled trains during the year, as are non-pass holding shareholders.

A variety of tickets are illustrated.

AUTHOR'S NOTE: Grateful thanks are due to Barney Forsdike for his invaluable assistance with this section.

Right: The Dowrick twins, Chris (left) and Colin, are seen at the Dunster ticket printing press.
Alain Lockyer

Commercial

The commercial operations of the company may be divided into two: the principal means of raising revenue is to sell train tickets, while useful and perhaps indispensable ancillaries are on-train catering and souvenir shops at several points along the railway.

Ticket offices

There are ticket offices at Minehead, Dunster, Blue Anchor, Watchet, Williton and Bishops Lydeard, all of which are normally staffed during the summer season but may be only staffed part-time outside that period. Passenger numbers from the remaining stations and halts, ie Washford, Doniford Beach Halt, Stogumber and Crowcombe Heathfield do not justify booking office facilities and passengers embarking from those stations are obliged to purchase their tickets on the train from either the guard or travelling ticket inspector.

Although Minehead continues to have the largest share of ticket sales, it now appears that the majority of passengers during the month of August commence their journey from the Bishops Lydeard end of the line. This initially put something of a strain on the facilities at that station, as mentioned above, which the new ticket office there has done much to alleviate.

From March to August 1976, Blue Anchor was the terminus of the line from Minehead. There were at that time no facilities in the station building, so tickets were sold from a small cabin at the Minehead end of the down platform. This cabin was affectionately known as 'The Tardis' and it may still be seen about the line.

Below: GWR 4-4-0 No 3440 *City of Truro* hauls the 'Victorian Belle', the 19.15 from Bishops Lydeard to Minehead, on 4 July 1992. *Stephen Edge*

Above: GWR 0-6-0 No 3205 at Bishops Lydeard at the head of the 'Quantock Belle'. John Pearce

Shops

For the 1976 reopening, the former parcels office at Minehead was converted into a shop and buffet. The latter was soon to prove inadequate and the facility moved elsewhere. The space thus vacated was then incorporated into the souvenir shop. It is, in any event, arguable whether refreshment facilities are required at Minehead in view of the numerous food and drink establishments only a short distance away. The shop's wares have expanded over the years and it is now possible to purchase small railway relics in addition to more common items. The shop at Minehead is the only one on the line operated by the company.

Most of the other stations, with the exception of Bishops Lydeard, sell limited numbers of souvenirs, mainly to support their station funds. Bishops Lydeard is in a slightly different league in that here the association has its main sales outlet. Although on a smaller scale than Minehead, there is a good selection of souvenirs, books, magazines and toys. The association relies quite heavily on the income generated by the shop at Bishops Lydeard and there is also a refreshment facility operating there under association auspices.

On-Train Catering

Even in the early days, experiments were conducted with refreshment trolleys on trains. This worked satisfactorily on sparsely-filled trains but was less successful during high summer in crowded coaches. At one time, too, refreshment facilities were provided in one of the DMU sets.

Recent years have seen much more stringent hygiene regulations being introduced and, of course, the railway has to comply with these as much as any other commercial organisation. To this end, one of the coaches was converted into a buffet car and met with such success that another one has also been converted. They are a real boon on a line of such length, when the journey one way can take over an hour and the round trip in excess of three hours, especially if there are small and fractious children to be entertained.

Refreshments available on trains include tea, coffee, soft drinks, beer, cider, sandwiches, chocolate and sweets, hot pies and pasties. New lines are constantly being tried with a view to extending the variety available.

'The Quantock Belle'

Undoubtedly the jewel in the crown of on-train catering on the WSR is the railway's dining train 'The Quantock Belle'. The train, which is entirely staffed by volunteers, caters for two sets of clientele: lunchers and diners. It runs perhaps two dozen times during the season and may be steam or diesel-hauled, although the evening trains are almost invariably steam-hauled from Bishops Lydeard, which is the start point. The train itself is privately owned, maintained and operated by the association. Seats are bookable in advance and needless to say, with its high reputation for quality and service, there is always a very long waiting list. It is often necessary to book months in advance, but it is also possible to travel on this train if one is not lunching or dining. Naturally, the fare for this is lower, but again it is necessary to book in advance.

Fares

Fares on the West Somerset Railway have always compared most favourably with those on similar lines. A comparative table is included to illustrate how fares on four other lines (two standard and two narrow gauge) compared for the 1995 season.

On reopening day, both service and fares were naturally of the most basic kind. This fortuitously made for ease of operation when dealing with the inevitably large crowds attracted by the opening of a new line. On 28 March 1976, only steam services were operated and there were none of the later complications arising when a two-tier fare structure was introduced for the diesel services. The original fares between Minehead and Blue

Anchor were 50p adult return and 30p child return (under 14).

Sample fares for the reopening to Williton on 28 August of that year were: adult return Minehead–Williton £1.30, to Watchet £1.10. Children under 14 were carried for 60p and 50p respectively.

Below: A few months before the line opened through to Bishops Lydeard, the 12.30 Minehead-Stogumber service leaves Williton on 31 March 1979 formed of one of the two two-car DMU sets. *Stephen Edge*

The next major revision came with the reopening to Bishops Lydeard on 9 June 1979. By this time the two-tier fare structure had got into its stride. Although steam train fares were noticeably more expensive than those for diesel travel, the best views were undoubtedly obtained from the units – and still are.

Sample fares for the new service were: adult return Minehead–Blue Anchor 90p; to Williton £1.70 and to Bishops Lydeard £2.70. Child returns for the same destinations were 55p, £1.00 and £1.50 respectively. Diesel multiple-unit fares, as stated, were cheaper, with the following on offer: Minehead–Watchet adult return 98p, child 65p; to Taunton £1.75 for adults and £1.15 for children.

Since the earliest days, the company has offered all manner of tickets at reduced rates. These have included the 'Starcard' scheme, special senior citizen rates, privilege rates for BR employees, party rates, special rates for disabled passengers and those accompanying them, Family rates, Rover tickets (both weekly and weekend) and a number of others. The Stored Journey Ticket has already been mentioned in the section on tickets.

The Family fare may be illustrated by giving rates in three widely-spaced years. In 1980, when the two-tier structure was still in place, it was £7.50 on the steam service. This covered two adults and two children. By 1988, this fare had risen to £12.50 and in 1995 it was £19.50.

In recent years, an 'Additional Child' ticket has been introduced. This is to cater for the family with more than two fare-paying children. It is purchased in conjunction with the Family Fare ticket at a cost of £1.00 per child up to a maximum of three.

Senior citizen rates are available also on all normal service trains. These are calculated at 20% of normal fares and apply to all trains except specials.

Party fares are an important part of the life of the Commercial Department and generous discounts are given for such advance bookings. It is necessary to make advance seat reservations for these bookings, since they may entail the addition of an extra coach to the normal service train.

Rover tickets have been introduced for full weeks and weekends. These have proved very popular, particularly when the company holds a Gala Weekend or something similar. Again, there are large discounts for these tickets; such a ticket from Minehead costs (1995) £31 for an adult (weekly) and £21 (weekend). For a child the figures were £15.50 and £10.50 respectively.

Half fares are charged for those between five and 15 years of age inclusive and under-fives travel free. Dogs are carried for 50p flat rate, regardless of distance travelled.

Although not part of the fares scheme, platform tickets are issued at some stations. With one exception, the income generated is treated effectively as donations and the tickets as souvenirs. The issuing stations are allocated a percentage for station funds. The exception is at Minehead during 'Friends of Thomas the Tank Engine' Weekends, when platform tickets are used for admission to the attractions, enabling some form of crowd control to be exercised. Those who subsequently decide to travel on the trains can have their tickets converted by paying the difference. These tickets are issued from a Setright machine on the platform or on the train.

FARES & DISTANCES – COMPARATIVE TABLE

LINE	ADULT RETURN	FAMILY RETURN	DISTANCE
North York Moors (Grosmont–Pickering)	£8.50	£21.90	18 miles
Severn Valley (Bridgnorth–Kidderminster)	£9.90†	£20.80	16 miles
Festiniog (Porthmadog–Blaenau Ffestiniog)	£11.60	£23.20	13½ miles
Isle of Man (Douglas–Port Erin)	£6.20	£18.60*	15½ miles
West Somerset (Minehead–Bishops Lydeard)	£7.70	£19.50	19½ miles

* The IoMR does not have a Family Ticket. Their equivalent is two adults and two children, ie £18.60.

† All return tickets between Kidderminster and Bridgnorth entitle the holder to unlimited travel over the whole line on the day of issue, except for the April and September Gala weekends, when special Rover tickets are available.

Staff and Personalities

Prior to the reopening of the line, the WSR, at that time still a private company, had no paid staff, all clerical and administrative work being done by volunteers. Practical work along the railway itself was also done by volunteers under the auspices of the association. All this was, perforce, to change from 28 March 1976.

Because staff salaries tend to form the bulk of any organisation's expenditure, paid staff of the company were kept to a minimum. Salaried staff then comprised a General Manager, Operating Superintendent, Locomotive Superintendent, Permanent Way Superintendent and Shop & Buffet Manageress.

The number of paid staff has fluctuated over the years, usually in accordance with the railway's financial position. End of season redundancies used to be a regular feature of life on the line for the staff and although seasonal staff are still employed for the summer, the permanent staff now have cause to feel more secure than at any time since 1976. Some of the present staff have been with the company for many years and have acquired a multitude of the skills so necessary to keep the numbers manageable.

Several names spring readily to mind: Operating Superintendent Steve Martin has been with the company full-time since 1986. However, he has been associated with the line both as a volunteer and part-time worker since well before reopening. He is qualified as a signalman, guard and DMU driver, but like many others will turn his hand to almost anything when the occasion demands. Ian Grady is another long-serving stalwart; like Steve Martin, a qualified signalman, guard and DMU driver, he has also acted as shop manager. Away from the railway, Ian is a Councillor for the Alcombe ward of Minehead Town Council. In the locomotive shed, Don Haynes and David Rouse have both been active as firemen, drivers and fitters since the mid-1970s. The latter is an acknowledged authority on rolling

stock, having at least one book to his credit.

Like any similar line, the West Somerset attracts its share of characters. The first Locomotive Superintendent (all appointments are based on those of the former Great Western Railway) was Harry Lee, a real one-off. He had worked in his youth for the old GWR and before the reopening had been Locomotive Officer for the association. He was principally responsible for the restoration of *Victor* and was the company's senior driver on reopening. Although no longer on the railway, he is still very much around and heavily involved with the return to steam of ex-GWR 2-6-2T No 5542, which is due to return to the line in the (hopefully) not-too-distant future.

The permanent staff have not had the monopoly of characters. In the early years the association had a member from Kent and East Sussex territory called Tom Waller, a delightful eccentric who used to tend the gardens at Stogumber station. He would appear at Williton station dressed in a kilt, wellington boots, floppy hat and old mackintosh, clutching his gardening tools, to catch the train to Stogumber. There he transformed what had been a wilderness into an attractive picnic area, laying the foundations for what it is today. Tom sold beansticks at the station to boost station funds. He died in 1987 and there is now a seat at Stogumber in his memory. Many older members will recall him with affection.

Not all the permanent staff are paid. The Commercial Manager is a volunteer, Hein Burger, lately a Commander in the Royal Netherlands Navy, who came to live in Minehead in 1980. Hein has given many years' loyal service to the railway, all of it unpaid.

Of course, the main workforce on the WSR consists of the volunteer members of the West Somerset Railway Association. At the time of writing, the association has around 4,500 members,

Left: Left to right: Dick Sloman, Steve Martin, Brian Hooper, Mark Smith, Brian Fisher, John Madeley, Major John Poyntz and Mick Phelps are seen during the HMRI inspection of Crowcombe Heathfield loop and signalling on 10 May 1994. *Norman Hawkes*

Right: Crowcombe stationmaster Walter Harris has obviously been to a car boot sale! *Peter Thompson*

of whom something like 400 may be active both on the railway and in other less obvious capacities. Many do more than one job; the last Editor of the *WSR Journal*, for example, is also a volunteer steam locomotive driver.

All the stations are staffed and largely maintained by volunteers; it would be impossible for things to be otherwise, if only on economic grounds. Among duties performed are signalman (at those stations with boxes), booking clerk, stationmasters, platform staff, painters and decorators, carpenters, builders, gardeners and people who come along to help in any way they can; and there is no shortage of work to be done.

A number of the WSR volunteers travel many miles at their own expense to give their services to the line.

Most important members of staff are the roster clerks, who, once again, usually double up in the jobs for which they perform this service. It is his (or her) task to allocate personnel to the jobs which must be filled if the service is to run smoothly. With a mainly volunteer organisation, this is by no means an easy task and relies heavily on people's goodwill. For most people, there is also a life away from the railway and there are not always many reserves to call upon in the event of someone becoming unavailable at short notice. At least three signalmen (and sometimes four) are required for every operating day. During high summer, as many as four two-man locomotive crews will be needed (and we do have some ladies as well); one round trip is considered sufficient in one day for any one crew. On special days, many more may be required. It should also be borne in mind that a driver only drives what he is passed to drive, particularly on the diesel side

Left: It's all hands on deck for the 'Friends of Thomas' events. Here John Glover and Rebecca Williams do their stuff on 13 June 1993. *Peter Thompson*

Right: Chairman of the West Somerset Railway Association, John Pearce, stands on the platform at Bishops Lydeard; ex-BR(W) 2-6-2T No 4160 forms the backdrop. *Stephen Edge*

and a steam driver will not necessarily (although he may) be qualified to drive a diesel locomotive or vice versa.

Every effort is made to staff all booking offices which sell tickets during the summer season. This considerably eases the burden on guards and travelling ticket inspectors, especially when trains are very full. For whatever reason, passengers on our line seem to wait till the very last minute and sometimes well beyond that before deciding whether to board a train or even buy a ticket!

Until the advent of the new booking office facilities at Bishops Lydeard, it was frequently necessary to get passengers on to trains without them being in possession of tickets, simply to enable trains to depart in reasonable time. Any long delays can cause havoc with the timetable, especially if the first trains of the day are late. The staff at Bishops Lydeard were fully extended in former days just keeping traffic on the move. Matters were complicated by the layout at this station and in particular by the barrow crossing at the north end, which was the quickest way to and from the ticket office, then in the station building. It says much for the sense of responsibility of the staff here that no serious accidents have ever occurred during stock movements.

This sense of responsibility has always been evident from the very earliest days. Running a railway is a very serious business and staff have always been alert to the almost suicidal tendencies to which some seem prone when on holiday. The West Somerset is not a large-scale train set and the company lays great emphasis on safe working at all times. Those who work on the line, in whatever capacity, have to satisfy management that they are competent in their chosen field.

At the time of writing, permanent staff are organised on the following lines: the Managing Director oversees the day-to-day running of the line on behalf of the board. In the locomotive department there is a Chief Locomotive Engineer with eight staff; the way and the works are overseen by the Civil Engineering Superintendent with six staff and the Signal Engineer, who is responsible for Signals and Telegraphs, co-ordinates the activities of about eight people at various times, mainly volunteers. The Commercial Manager, himself a volunteer, is responsible for those members of staff, many of them being volunteers, who work in the shop at Minehead and in the buffet cars on trains. He also looks after booking clerks. All told, the permanent staff numbers about two dozen, while a few extra staff may be taken on for the summer season. As can be imagined, the number of volunteer staff varies from day to day. It is quite possible that there may be as many as 60, or even more, at various points along the line in high summer.

There is a constant requirement for volunteers in all departments. All are welcome, young and old, male and female, and every effort is made to find suitable jobs for all commensurate with his or her wishes and abilities. Any persons wishing to offer their services are asked to contact the Enquiry Office at Minehead station in the first instance, from where their enquiries will be passed on to the Volunteer Co-ordinator or appropriate Head of Department. No previous experience is necessary, although anyone with specialist railway skills will naturally be made especially welcome.

One of the West Somerset Railway's claims to fame is having someone thought to be the oldest active railwayman in the country. This is Harry Horn. Now stationmaster at Stogumber, Harry started work with the *original* Great Western Railway just after World War 1 and eventually became signalman at Williton in BR days. He continues to take an active and lively interest in happenings on the line, despite now being confined more or less permanently to a wheelchair. He is ably supported by his wife of 60 years, Iris, and the pair of them greet nearly all visitors, passengers and trains at their station. Harry celebrated his 90th birthday in 1994.

Chapter 13

Other Attractions along the Line

Over the years, a number of attractions have sprung up along the line, all in keeping with the company's aim of creating a working Great Western Railway branch line. With space at Minehead being at a premium, there is little at the station. In any event, the town holds attractions of its own; nevertheless, a coach containing a model railway layout is to be found at the promenade end of the station. It is situated next to the carriage which provides the station's refreshments and is open at most operating times.

The former waiting room on the down platform at Blue Anchor now houses a remarkable museum of small artefacts relating mainly but not exclusively to the Great Western Railway. It is well worth a visit and there is no admission charge although, of course, donations are always most welcome. Amongst other things, one may have the opportunity to try out a ticket printing press of the same type as that used at Dunster for producing WSR and other tickets. The Blue Anchor Railway Museum was created by the West Somerset Steam Railway Trust and is maintained and staffed by its members on most operating days during high summer and weekends outside that period.

At the next station, Washford, the Somerset & Dorset Railway Trust has also created an interesting museum and shed complex. This, as its name implies, is devoted to the former Somerset & Dorset Joint Railway, whose main line ran between Bath and Bournemouth and was closed completely in 1966. The Trust owns 2-8-0 No 53808, which is one of the locomotives in regular use on the WSR. Again, all visitors are made most welcome, as are

donations towards the work of the Trust. Among its activities is a reunion weekend at Washford every other year for former employees of the Somerset & Dorset, which is always well attended. Special trains are run and there are additional attractions at the station. The layout here has been created since 1976 from a greenfield site.

Crowcombe Heathfield station has an interesting exhibition of permanent way materials on the down platform. The exhibit includes a section of broad gauge track with which, until 1882, the West Somerset Railway was laid. The point-lever displayed is also a broad gauge relic. Several of the smaller exhibits, like the milepost, may be seen along the line.

As already mentioned, Bishops Lydeard now has a Visitor Centre, created from the former goods shed. The whole character of this station has changed since its use was changed to that of a terminal station. In former days, when it was just another passing place on the line, there was no requirement to provide interest for passengers waiting for trains. However, the present administration recognises the need to provide additional attractions for passengers awaiting trains, and in particular for younger members of the family, whose boredom threshold may be low! Inside the Centre is usually displayed, amongst smaller objects, a historic locomotive or item of rolling stock. At the time of writing, this is a carriage from the Royal Train of the Great Western Railway. It was designated for use by Her Majesty Queen Elizabeth, The Queen Mother and is on loan from the National Railway Museum at York.

Left: A rake of DMUs is captured at Stogumber station on 29 May 1978. The late Tom Waller stands on the right outside the station building. *John Reeves*

The West Somerset Railway Association

The West Somerset Railway Association was formed in 1971 with its principal objective the reopening of the branch line between Taunton and Minehead. It is of some interest that the association was formed before the company.

In common with the supporters' organisations on other railways, the association and its members have been directly responsible from the very beginning both for the provision of a major portion of the labour essential to the running of the line and equally important, though not so widely known, regular injections of large amounts of cash. This latter was of considerable importance in the late 1970s and early 1980s, when the fortunes of the company were at a particularly low ebb.

There have always been very close links between association and company. Many, if not most, association members are also shareholders in the company and many shareholders are members of the association. The association is well represented on the board by several of its officers and, similarly, some directors hold positions on the association committee. Thus it may be said that with such close liaison, room for misunderstanding is lessened and common goals are more easily achieved.

Once the line was reopened, it was possible to offer more in the way of concessions to association members than just a monthly newsletter and with the advent of the *Journal* in 1978, all association members were offered a high-quality quarterly magazine, travel concessions on the line and the chance, if so desired, to work on the railway. The 1995 concession is two days' unlimited free travel, except on days when special timetables operate. This may be said to be equal to two Day Rover tickets, currently valued at £25.

It will be appreciated that it costs an enormous amount of money to run a large railway such as the West Somerset, since even in winter staff have to be paid to do essential maintenance not possible when the trains are running; also ongoing bills have to be met. Consequently, the support provided by the association and its members is vital and very much appreciated by the company. Any reader who feels he or she would like to assist in the task is cordially invited to write for details of membership to:

The Membership Secretary
West Somerset Railway Association
The Railway Station
Bishops Lydeard
TAUNTON
Somerset   TA4 3BX

Below: No 3205, an ex-GWR 0-6-0, is pictured near Black Monkey Bridge on 11 September 1988 with the 12.15 Minehead-Bishops Lydeard service. *Stephen Edge*

West Somerset Steam Railway Trust *Ian Coleby*

The trust was initially formed at the same time as the company with the intention of being a charitable body which would buy the trackbed from the council. There may also have been an intention to acquire some rolling stock, although this never happened.

After the trackbed purchase fell through, the trust largely became dormant, though a very small number of members continued to pay regular contributions. However, in 1984, principally at the instigation of member Graham Stagg, then Editor of the *WSR Journal*, the trust was relaunched, primarily to ensure that the money which had been accrued up to that time was properly spent.

This was a time of great financial hardship for the company and it was intended that money should be contributed towards returning No 4561 to service, in order to assist the company in a practical way. At the same time, Blue Anchor Railway Museum (BARM) was opened entirely as a trust project and since 1985 the trust has maintained the museum in its primary position. During the first year of opening, the museum attracted 2,800 visitors over 43 days.

Other projects have included practical financial assistance towards the return to service of No 4160 (the trust is a major shareholder) and perhaps most notably the restoration of ex-GWR sleeping car No 9038 of 1897 vintage. Further projects are in the pipeline.

The trust keeps an eye on the historical aspects of the railway and offers the company suggestions, criticism and comments on how best to retain the period atmosphere. The trust is always pleased to hear from prospective members and contact may be made through:

The Secretary, West Somerset Steam Railway Trust, The Railway Station, Williton, Somerset TA4 4RQ.

Ian Coleby is the Archivist to the West Somerset Steam Railway Trust

GWR record breaker No 3440 *City of Truro* is caught outside the Visitor Centre at Bishops Lydeard during 1992. The ex-GWR first-class sleeping car, dating from 1898, stands in the platform road. *John Pearce*

The Somerset & Dorset Railway Trust *John Simms*

The link between the Somerset & Dorset Railway Trust and the West Somerset Railway was born of the collapse, for a variety of reasons, of the trust's attempt to establish a preservation scheme at Radstock. This folded in the mid-1970s and the trust looked at a number of possibilities before deciding that the West Somerset project offered the best prospects for the future.

The trust was offered a couple of possible station sites but selected Washford by reason of the large area of the former goods yard. Although this was weed-grown and track-free with the buildings long gone, Washford's former cattle market traffic had meant that this small station could offer scope for a sizeable restoration base. Within a few weeks of the agreement being signed, the trust's volunteers were on site and the scene at Washford was described as 'resembling a battlefield' as preparations for track-laying began. This phase passed, but not before friction had arisen between the trust and local residents over the blotting of the landscape!

From the late 1970s to date, work has progressed in a steady but significant manner. Track has been laid to give a large fan of sidings and in the late 1980s money was found to enable contractors to build a large restoration shed. A museum of Somerset & Dorset relics is established in the station building and the original Washford signalbox has been fitted out internally as a replica of the one-time Midford box. For many years, the museum opened on Sundays, Bank Holidays and daily in August but in recent times, this has expanded to all WSR operating days between March and the end of October.

In many ways, the trust has shared the vicissitudes and triumphs of the WSR. Old hands can recall affixing certificates of ownership to everything

Below: Restored to Somerset & Dorset Joint Railway livery, No 88 is seen at the Bishops Lydeard water tower on 10 August 1992. *Stephen Edge*

in sight in the dark days of the early 1980s, when the Official Receiver seemed due, but the biggest example of co-operation is the '7F' 2-8-0 locomotive. This had been bought by the trust in the Radstock days and work had been done on it, but the move to Washford meant a loss of momentum. Working parties grew fewer in number and working in the open air was often miserable and unproductive. Finally, the trust decided that the only way to get the engine back into action was to put the job out to contract. Four offers were received, including one from the WSR.

At that stage in its history, the West Somerset had little pedigree in locomotive overhaul and prudence suggested going elsewhere. However, the WSR was clearly rapidly turning the corner in its own fortunes and the trust had a gut feeling that the engine should remain linked with Somerset. The contract was placed, faith was magnificently justified and the big, black freight engine has given doggedly faithful service on heavy trains for almost a decade since 1987. One of the ironies is that some turns on the WSR in the peak service involve greater mileage than No 88's original freight diagrams over the Mendips.

The trust also has a good-sized collection of wagons, some of which were passed for working in West Somerset Railway demonstration freight trains and can otherwise be viewed in the Washford sidings. One of the more useful items in the collection is the 1908 steam crane. Formerly at the works of Stothert & Pitt in Bath, this was for a long time the most powerful crane on the West Somerset and was used for various heavy lifts, such as the removal of the train heating boiler from 'Hymek' No D7017 after the locomotive had hauled the '7F' to Washford.

Other major artefacts in the trust's possession include the former Burnham-on-Sea signalbox, the Goods Office from Wells and the goods shed crane from Binegar. In 1986, the body of coach No 4, built in 1890, was obtained and work has been proceeding steadily on its restoration. In 1994, two more carriage bodies of similar vintage were acquired and the creation of a Victorian train will form a major part of the trust's activities in the coming years.

The relationship between trust and railway has been generally beneficial and largely harmonious. The down side is that volunteers tend to go for the bigger concern and, as a result, the Washford workforce has remained dedicated but small. The major plus point is that association with the thriving railway keeps visitor numbers and interest higher than would be the case at an isolated museum. Above all, when '7F' No 88 comes round the curve and up the bank into Washford at the head of a holiday train, something of the old 'Dorset spirit' lives on.

John Simms is Press Officer to the Somerset & Dorset Railway Trust

Diesel & Electric Preservation Group *Don Bishop*

Back in 1972, when the first of the BR Western Region's diesel-hydraulic locomotives were withdrawn from active service, a small group of enthusiasts got together and decided to purchase a Class 42 'Warship' locomotive for preservation. This was a brave step, as no main line diesel had been preserved at that time; most enthusiasts were still mourning the end of steam just four years previously and getting support for the project was likely to prove difficult. After a while, sufficient funds had been raised for BR to be persuaded to sell Class 42 No D821 *Greyhound* to the group, which

Below: 'Western' class diesel-hydraulic No D1035 *Western Yeoman* double-heads with 'Warship' class No D821 *Greyhound* a service train arriving at Crowcombe Heathfield on 28 October 1991. Don Bishop occupies the Second Man position. *Peter Thompson*

later went on to become the Diesel Traction Group. As 1975 approached, other appeals had been started to purchase 'Western' and 'Hymek' diesel-hydraulics and it was one of these groups, which was attempting to purchase a Class 35 'Hymek', that became the Diesel & Electric Group, as it was then known. At that time, the West Somerset Railway was in the early stages of revival and the group negotiated with the company to bring their loco to the line.

The group was successful in the purchase of No D7017 from BR for £3,500 and the locomotive was moved to Taunton for storage with various other items of rolling stock awaiting transfer to the WSR when the Light Railway Order had been obtained. No D7017 was not the group's first choice; No D7026 was considered to be in better overall condition. However, the latter was returned to traffic by BR for use on engineers' trains in connection with the upgrading of the West of England main line for

125mph High Speed Trains. As a result, it was considered that its 'engine hours' would be rather high at the end of this work and No D7017 was chosen instead. The locomotive was moved on to the WSR and saw only occasional use in the early years, as its axle loading was now deemed too heavy for the line – despite regular workings by the class to Minehead in BR days.

Meanwhile, another 'Hymek', No D7018, was based at Didcot Railway Centre, having been purchased privately. Its owner later decided that he wished to sell the locomotive and bid for a Class 52 'Western'. Terms were agreed and the D&EG purchased the locomotive for £3,600 as a source of spares for No D7017. However, the loco was found to be in rather good condition, so it was decided to restore it rather than use it as spares.

Several years passed with the group working as two separate operations: one at Didcot and the other at Williton, which had now become the permanent base of the group on the West Somerset Railway. In 1979, the group was fortunate to be given a Class 14 diesel-hydraulic shunter by the Westbury Cement Works for use on the WSR. No D9526 required extensive restoration after its industrial use in the cement works and this work was carried out by D&EG members at Williton. Around this time, a group of individuals also purchased another Class 14, No D9551, from Ashington in Northumberland and this loco was also based at the group's depot at Williton. With the completion of overhauls on these two locomotives, the group was able to supply the West Somerset Railway with diesel motive power as required.

Restoration work continued at Williton on No D7017, which still saw occasional use on special workings over the line, and on No D7018 at Didcot. During the early 1980s, when the WSR was in financial difficulties, the group purchased one of the company's two Park Royal DMU sets and after some

minor attention, hired it back to the company for further use on the line. Another D&EG member purchased a Rolls-Royce-engined Sentinel shunter from Staveley Steel Works and this was put to use as depot pilot at Williton.

In 1985, the group's current chairman, Bob Tiller, approached quarry giants Foster Yeoman about taking on the full restoration of 'Western' No D1010 *Western Campaigner*, which that company had bought and renumbered/renamed to D1035 *Western Yeoman*, with the intention of mounting it on a plinth outside its premises near Frome. The original No D1035 was unavailable to it owing to damage sustained just prior to withdrawal from BR traffic. Planning permission to place the 'Western' on its plinth was refused by Mendip District Council and the locomotive remained at Merehead in open storage for some nine years. Terms were agreed for the locomotive to go on long-term loan to the D&EG and it was moved to Didcot for restoration.

As the group's fleet had expanded by the late 1980s, it was decided to apply for registered charity status and change the name to Diesel & Electric Preservation Group Ltd.

Work was undertaken on No D7017 around 1989 to reduce its axle weight to within the line's 17½-ton limit and thus enable the locomotive to work more often. Around this time, also, it was becoming obvious that the group working at two different locations, Didcot and Williton, was becoming a problem and as the Great Western Society at Didcot had indicated that they intended to have a steam-only depot, the group decided to move out and concentrate its efforts at Williton.

Firstly, the 'Western' was moved from Didcot to its owners' base at Merehead for storage over Christmas 1990 and thence on to the WSR. This movement was sponsored by Foster Yeoman, which used its own Class 59 locomotives for the moves. The 'Western' made its début on the WSR later in 1991 in desert

Right: Western Yeoman's two Maybach diesel engines are pictured in the shed at Williton on 28 February 1993. D&EPG Treasurer Dave Pike ponders his next move. Peter Thompson

sand livery, which looked particularly smart with the chocolate and cream coaches.

'Hymek' No D7018 remained at Didcot until later that year, when it moved to Old Oak Common, London, for display at an Open Day and thence on to Laira (Plymouth) for another Open Day before arriving at the WSR in late September 1991. This effected the move of No D7018 at no cost.

A problem arose in 1989, when blue asbestos was found in the Park Royal DMU. The set was withdrawn from service, along with the company's DMU fleet whilst it was decided what action should be taken. The D&EPG hired its Class 14 No D9526 to the company to cover diagrams at this time and this loco operated alongside No D9551, which had now been purchased by the company. Subsequently, the group spent £9,000 on having the asbestos stripped from the unit by a specialist company under controlled conditions. At the time of writing, the unit is part-way through a major rebuild following this work and it is hoped to have it back in service in the not-too-distant future.

With the weight reduction works having been completed on both 'Hymeks' and the 'Western' coming within the line's axle loading, the group's fleet started to see much more use and today the D&EPG is seen as the company's sole provider of diesel locomotives for passenger trains. The group was able to hold two very successful Diesel Gala Days in 1992 and 1993, with visiting locomotives, one of which was loaned by BR and became the first BR locomotive to work to Minehead for nearly 20 years.

Early in 1994, the D&EPG was approached by the Class 50 Society, which was looking for a home for their Class 50 No 50149 *Defiance*. Although the locomotive was actually too heavy for regular use on the line at that time, special permission might be sought for a limited number of runs over the line due to ongoing upgrading works by the company. Terms were agreed and the Class 50 joined the fleet in

May 1994. Later that summer, a group member obtained Class 08 shunter No 08850 from BR and this locomotive joined the fleet at Williton. The group had also taken on ownership of the 'Western' by this time, having purchased it from Foster Yeoman for the princely sum of £1!

With the ability to get special permission to run bigger locomotives on the line, the opportunity was taken to hold a bigger Diesel Gala in 1994 and the group turned out its own fleet of six locomotives and two visitors: No D1062 *Western Courier* and No D821 *Greyhound*, both now based on the Severn Valley Railway. The event was the most successful gala ever operated, of any sort, on the WSR. A similar event was staged in 1995.

The D&EPG has now matured to become the 'elder statesman' of diesel preservation and is enjoying a firm and fruitful relationship with the WSR as a major part of their operations. The group has now signed a 35-year sub-lease with the company for its Williton depot site and is currently building a new two-road engine shed at the site to protect its fleet from the elements and for future generations to see what these vintage diesels look like.

From its early beginnings at the very outset of diesel preservation, the group is now leading the way as a professional organisation operating on a real railway. Regular working parties are held at Williton and anyone who wishes to become involved can contact the group at:

Diesel & Electric Preservation Group Ltd
The Locomotive Depot
Williton Goods Yard
Williton
Somerset
TA4 4RQ

Don Bishop is Press Officer to the Diesel & Electric Preservation Group

Appendices

WEST SOMERSET RAILWAY PLC

General Managers
David Butcher
Anthony Griffiths
Christopher van den Arend
(Administrative Director)
Leonard Clark
Douglas Hill

Managing Directors
Douglas Fear
Peter Rivett
Mark Smith

WEST SOMERSET RAILWAY PLC

Chairmen
Douglas Fear
Richard Stevens
Derek Portman
David Morgan
Dennis Taylor

Below: Newly outshopped, the flagship of the D&EPG's fleet, 'Hymek' No D7017, is seen at Williton on 5 September 1993. *Peter Thompson*

BIBLIOGRAPHY

The West Somerset Railway: A History in Pictures. C. R. Clinker. Exmoor Press. Various editions from 1980.

Transport of Delight. Cedric Dunmall. Exmoor Press, 1990.

West Somerset Railway (No 8 in 'Steam Portfolio' series). Richard Jones. Ian Allan, 1992.

Railways Round Exmoor. Robin Madge. Exmoor Press. Various editions.

Branch Line to Minehead. Vic Mitchell & Keith Smith. Middleton Press, 1990.

The Taunton to Minehead Railway. Published by Minehead Round Table, 1970.

The First Five Years of the West Somerset Railway. Published by West Somerset Books, 1981.

The West Somerset Railway Guide Book.

The West Somerset Railway Stations & Buildings Book.

The West Somerset Railway Stock Book. West Somerset Railway Association Newsletters 1971–77.

West Somerset Railway Journals 1978–95.